CALCULUS

FOR EVERYONE

EXERCISE SOLUTIONS AND ANSWER KEY

EXERCISE SOLUTIONS
AND ANSWER KEY

CALCULUS
FOR EVERYONE

UNDERSTANDING PHYSICS
AND THE MATHEMATICS
OF CHANGE

MITCH STOKES

WITH ILLUSTRATIONS BY SUMMER STOKES

Calculus for Everyone: Exercise Solutions and Answer Key, by Mitch Stokes

Illustrations by Summer Stokes.

Published by Roman Roads Press
121 E. 3rd Street, Moscow, Idaho 83843
romanroadspress.com

Cover design by Rachel Rosales.

Printed in the United States of America.

ISBN-13: 978-1-944482-55-8
ISBN-10: 1-944482-55-5

Version 2.2.1 | February 2025

CONTENTS

SCHEDULES

32-WEEK SCHEDULE

WEEK	TEXT	VIDEO
1	How to Use This Book and Preface	How to Use This Book (16 min.) and Preface + Introduction (17 min.)
2	Chapter 1, Study Questions	Lecture 1: The Problem of Change (18 min.)
3	Chapter 2, Study Questions	Lecture 2: Space, Time & Number (19 min.)
4	Chapter 3, Study Questions	Lecture 3: The Paradox of Speed (20 min.)
5	Chapter 4, Study Questions, Exercises	Lecture 4: The Platonic-Pythagorian Project Before the Scientific Revolution—Part I (21 min.) and Part II (22 min.)
6	Chapter 5, Study Questions, Exercises	Lecture 5: The Scientific Revolution and the Need for Calculus (46 min.)
7	Chapter 6, Study Questions	Lecture 6: Newton and Calculus (42 min.)
8	Chapter 7, Study Questions	Lecture 7: The Essential Tools—Variables, Functions & Graphs (51 min.)

Week	Reading	Lecture
9	Chapter 8, Study Questions & Exercises	Lecture 8: A New Tool—The Limit (41 min.)
10	**Take Exam 1: Chapters 1–8**	———
11	Chapter 9, Study Questions & Exercises	Lecture 9: The Method of Approximation and Defining Instantaneous Speed (41 min.)
12	Chapter 10, Study Questions & Exercises	Lecture 10: Using the Method of Increments to Calculate Instantaneous Speed (45 min.)
13	Chapter 11, Study Questions & Exercises	Lecture 11: Using the Method of Increments to Find an Instantaneous Speed Function (30 min.)
14	Chapter 12, Study Questions & Exercises	Lecture 12: The Derivative (50 min.)
15	Chapter 13, Study Questions & Exercises	Lecture 13: Finding More Derivatives (43 min.)
16	Chapter 14, Study Questions & Exercises	Lecture 14: Using the Power Rule to Find Derivatives (38 min.)
17	**Take Exam 2: Chapters 9–14**	———
18	Chapter 15, Study Questions & Exercises	Lecture 15: Derivatives and the Problem of Change, Part I and II (74 min.)
19	Chapter 16, Study Questions	Lecture 16: Graphs and Slopes (49 min.)
20	Chapter 17, Study Questions & Exercises	Lecture 17: Slopes and Derivatives (38 min.)
21	Chapter 18, Study Questions & Exercises	Lecture 18: Slopes and the Problem of Change (29 min.)

22	Chapter 19, Study Questions & Exercises	Lecture 19: More Information from Derivatives (46 min.)
23	Chapter 20, Study Questions & Exercises	Lecture 20: Looking Closer at Graphs of Free Fall (41 min.)
24	**Take Exam 3: Chapters 15–20**	
25	Chapter 21, Study Questions & Exercises	Lecture 21: The Anti-Derivative—Undoing Derivatives (49 min.)
26	Chapter 22, Study Questions	Lecture 22: Defining the Integral (38 min.)
27	Chapter 23, Study Questions	Lecture 23: Using the Method of Summation to Calculate Integrals, Part I (28 min.)
28	Chapter 23, Exercises	Lecture 23: Using the Method of Summation to Calculate Integrals, Part II (69 min.)
29	Chapter 24, Study Questions & Exercises	Lecture 24: The Fundamental Theorem of Calculus (38 min.)
30	Chapter 25, Study Questions & Exercises	Lecture 25: Interpreting Areas (37 min.)
31	Epilogue	Epilogue, Part I and II (85 min.)
32	**Comprehensive Final Exam**	

16-WEEK SCHEDULE

WEEK	TEXT	VIDEO
1	How to Use This Book, Preface, Chapter 1, and Chapter 2	How to Use This Book, Preface, and Introduction (24 min.) Lecture 1: The Problem of Change (18 min.) Lecture 2: Space, Time & Number (19 min.)
2	Chapter 3, Chapter 4, and Chapter 5	Lecture 3: The Paradox of Speed (20 min.) Lecture 4: The Platonic-Pythagorian Project Before the Scientific Revolution—Part I (21 min.) and Part II (22 min.) Lecture 5: The Scientific Revolution and the Need for Calculus (23 min.)
3	Chapter 6, Chapter 7, and Chapter 8	Lecture 6: Newton and Calculus (24 min.) Lecture 7: The Essential Tools—Variables, Functions & Graphs (25 min.) Lecture 8: A New Tool—The Limit (26 min.)
4	**Take Exam 1: Chapters 1–8**	
5	Chapter 9 and Chapter 10	Lecture 9: The Method of Approximation and Defining Instantaneous Speed (27 min.) Lecture 10: Using the Method of Increments to Calculate Instantaneous Speed (28 min.)
6	Chapter 11 and Chapter 12	Lecture 11: Using the Method of Increments to Find an Instantaneous Speed Function (29 min.) Lecture 12: The Derivative (30 min.)
7	Chapter 13 and Chapter 14	Lecture 13: Finding More Derivatives (31 min.) Lecture 14: Using the Power Rule to Find Derivatives (38 min.)
8	**Take Exam 2: Chapters 9–14**	

9	Chapter 15, Parts I and II, and Chapter 16	Lecture 15: Derivatives and the Problem of Change—Part I (32 min.) and Part II (42 min.) Lecture 16: Graphs and Slopes (49 min.)
10	Chapter 17 and Chapter 18	Lecture 17: Slopes and Derivatives (38 min.) Lecture 18: Slopes and the Problem of Change (29 min.)
11	Chapter 19 and Chapter 20	Lecture 19: More Information from Derivatives (46 min.) Lecture 20: Looking Closer at Graphs of Free Fall (44 min.)
12	**Take Exam 3: Chapters 15–20**	———
13	Chapter 21 and Chapter 22	Lecture 21: The Anti-Derivative—Undoing Derivatives (49 min.) Lecture 22: Defining the Integral (38 min.)
14	Chapter 23, Parts I and II	Lecture 23: Using the Method of Summation to Calculuate Integrals, Part I (28 min.) and Part II (69 min.)
15	Chapter 24, Chapter 25, and Epilogue, Parts I and II	Lecture 25: Using the Method of Increments to Find an Instantaneous Speed Function (37 min.) Epilogue—Part I: The Problem of Change (47 min.) and Part II: Zeno's Paradox (38 min.)
16	**Comprehensive Final Exam**	———

ANSWERS TO THE STUDY QUESTIONS & EXERCISE SOLUTIONS

CHAPTER 1 - THE PROBLEM OF CHANGE

ANSWERS TO THE STUDY QUESTIONS

1. What is *the problem of change*?

   The problem of change can be summed up in a simple question: why do things change?

2. Briefly explain how the problem of change inaugurated Western philosophy.

   The problem of change inaugurated Western philosophy by setting man on a quest to understand the world which is a teeming mass of change and motion.

3. What is the problem of motion?

   The problem of motion is another name for the problem of change.

4. Briefly explain why orderliness is important to the problem of change.

   Order is important to the problem of change because change is frequently tidy and organized, even though the world is so often prone to disorder.

5. Give your own example(s) of motion or change that is not orderly.

   Answers will vary.
   A hurricane tears through a community.

6. Give your own example(s) of motion or change that is orderly.

   Answers will vary.
   The seasons return each year and in the same order.

7. What is "natural philosophy"?

   "Natural philosophy" is the philosophy of nature or what we now call "science."

8. What was Thales' answer to the problem of change? How was this answer a step forward in answering the problem?

   Thales answer to the problem of change was that everything is made of water. His answer was a step forward in answering the problem because he put the problem of change on the table and gave the world a sample solution.

9. When did Thales live (very roughly)?

   Thales lived circa 500s BC.

10. There are two main reason why Thales is important to Western philosophy. What are they?

    The two main ways in which Thales was important are: first, he set the agenda for Western philosophy with his attempt to explain why the world around us changes while maintaining so much order; and second, he was the first mathematician (the first person to try to systematically prove mathematical statements).

11. What was the Pythagorean motto? Explain what this motto means. (Hint: how did Morris Kline unpack the motto?)

    The Pythagorean motto was "All is number." This motto has three underlying ideas: first, that the universe is ordered according to perfect mathematical laws, second, that divine reason is the orderer, and third, that human reason can discern the divine mathematical pattern.

12. When did Pythagoras live (very roughly)?

    Pythagoras lived circa 500s BC.

13. What Pythagorean discovery led to the Pythagorean motto?

The Pythagorean discovery that led to the Pythagorean motto was the discovery that musical intervals could be represented by whole numbers. In other words, it was discovered that simple mathematics could describe something as seemingly nonmathematical as music.

14. What is the music of the spheres? Why were the Pythagoreans impressed by the connection between music and mathematics? Why do you think that we aren't usually impressed by this?

    The Pythagoreans believed that the motion of the heavenly bodies (the sun, moon, planets, and stars) produced actual harmonic music which is called "the music of the spheres."

    The Pythagoreans were impressed by the connection between music and mathematics because there is no apparent reason for the math to work out so nicely when it comes to music and the vibration of strings. I think that we aren't usually impressed by this because we are so used to using numbers to describe things—music, velocity, weight, density, etc.—we entirely expect the world to help us out like this.

15. When we say that mathematics applies to the world, what do we mean exactly? (Hint: what two realms are similar?)

    When we say that mathematics applies to the world, we mean that math, although it is nonphysical, can accurately describe the world, even though the world is physical.

16. What did Wigner say about the applicability of mathematics to the physical world? Why couldn't he make sense of why math "works"? How did Plato make sense of it?

    Wigner said that "The miracle of the appropriateness of the language of mathematics for the formulation of the laws of physics is a wonderful gift which we neither understand nor deserve." In other words, he said we cannot understand why Math "works." He couldn't make sense of why math "works" because he was not aware that the universe was created by an intelligent designer, a God who is a mathematician. Plato made sense of the applicability of

math by saying that the world *is* mathematical, and he believed that the world was mathematical because God made it that way.

17. What two important views did Plato inherit from the Pythagoreans?

    The two important views that Plato inherited from the Pythagoreans were that the human soul is immortal, and that the physical world is fundamentally mathematical.

18. According to Plato, humans are divided into two very different kinds of things. What are these two things?

    According to Plato, humans are composed of two parts: a physical body and a nonphysical soul or mind.

19. Plato divided reality into two main realms. Explain.

    Plato divided reality into two main realms: the physical realm and the non-physical realm. The physical part is just the ordinary universe we live in. The nonphysical part is a world of *Ideas* or *Forms*.

20. How do Plato's two "worlds" correspond to the two parts of humans?

    The physical part of humans', the physical body, corresponds to the physical world, whereas the nonphysical part of humans', the soul or mind, corresponds to the nonphysical world.

21. What is "Plato's Heaven"?

    "Plato's Heaven" is the mysterious, nonphysical "realm" or "world" where the Ideas or Forms exist.

22. What are Forms?

    Forms are actual nonphysical objects that literally exist outside the physical world, independent of any minds. They are absolutely perfect, they exist eternally, and they never, ever change.

23. Explain how, according to Plato, the physical world is a mere copy. Be sure to give an example.

The physical world is a mere copy of the nonphysical world because the perfect blueprints for things in the world are found in the nonphysical world, and when these things are found in the world, they are never perfect, they can cease to exist, and they can change. For example, the perfect Idea of Circularity exists in Plato's Heaven, but circles in the world are never perfectly circular. (Examples may vary.)

24. What is Plato's answer for why the world is mathematical?

    Plato's answer for why the world is mathematical is that God made it that way. Plato's "god" used the mathematical forms and so the world too is mathematical.

25. According to Plato, why was the study of mathematics important?

    Plato believed that our souls are more important than our bodies. According to Plato it is important to take care of our souls, to purify them. For Plato, the soul is purified by becoming more like the Forms, more like the eternal, perfect Ideas that inhabit Plato's heaven. The way to do this, said Plato, is to study mathematics.

26. Explain how Plato's *Republic* is important in the history of the liberal arts. What does this have to do with Pythagoras?

    The education that Plato sketches in his book the *Republic* is where the West gets the notion of the *liberal arts*. There are seven liberal arts and four of them, the *quadrivium* (arithmetic, geometry, astronomy, and music) were handed down to Plato by the Pythagoreans.

27. What is the "music of the spheres"?

    The Pythagoreans believed that the motion of the heavenly bodies (the sun, moon, planets, and stars) produced actual harmonic music which is called "the music of the spheres."

28. What was the homework that Plato assigned the Academy? Why is this assignment historically important?

    For homework, Plato wanted the Academy to create a mathematical system that accurately described and predicted the motion of the heavens. This is

historically important because it brings us back to the problem of change—this time the motion of the sun, moon, planets, and stars in all their bewildering meanderings. He wanted to tackle the problem of change in the physical world using mathematics.

29. How did Plato attack the problem of change? That is what was his version of the problem?

    Plato's version of the problem dealt with the motion of the heavenly bodies, the physical world, and he believed the problem could be solved using mathematics. Whereas Thales tackled the problem of change by saying that everything is made of water, Plato attacked the problem by saying that everything can be described mathematically.

30. Why is Plato's problem of change so difficult to solve?

    Plato's problem of change is so difficult to solve because he wanted to describe the motion of the sun, moon, stars, and planets (the entire cosmos) mathematically. It is even more difficult to solve because the heavenly bodies don't really move in an orderly fashion.

CHAPTER 2 - SPACE, TIME, AND NUMBERS

ANSWERS TO THE STUDY QUESTIONS

1. What is Plato's challenge?

   Plato's challenge is to mathematically describe the apparently chaotic motion of the heavens.

2. What are two of the difficulties with describing motion using mathematics? There is another difficulty. What is it?

   One difficulty with describing motion using mathematics is the sheer difficulty of discovering the exact mathematics to describe the universe's mathematical order. The other difficulty is the deep conceptual problems surrounding the very idea of motion. Another difficulty has to do with the basic concepts related to motion: space, time, numbers, and speed.

3. What was the philosophical controversy that sparked Zeno's paradox?

   The philosophical controversy that sparked Zeno's paradox was a controversy between Heraclitus and Parmenides that had to do with how they viewed change. Heraclitus, on the one hand, believed that *everything* changes. On the other hand, Parmenides believed that nothing whatsoever changes and that the very concept of change is incoherent.

4. Very roughly, when did Zeno live?

   Zeno lived circa 400s BC.

5. What was Zeno's outrageous suggestion? What was his argument for this?

   Zeno's outrageous suggestion was that motion simply can't occur. He argued that, in order to traverse any distance, you would first have to traverse half of it. But to traverse half the distance, you would first need to traverse half of that distance (a quarter of the original distance). Zeno said that we could continue dividing distances forever, meaning that we would need to traverse an infinite number of distances which would take an infinite amount of time—an

eternity. Since traversing any distance would mean traversing an infinite number of distances in an infinite amount of time, Zeno concluded that motion was impossible.

6. Of course, you don't believe Zeno's suggestion. So what is the real problem that Zeno's paradox poses for us? In other words, what does Zeno's paradox rightly point out to us?

   The real problem that Zeno's paradox poses for us is that motion is a difficult concept to analyze or define. Zeno's paradox rightly points out to us that we need to be able to precisely define *motion*.

7. What is Aristotle's little motto about motion and nature?

   Aristotle's little motto about motion and nature is, "Ignorance of motion is ignorance of nature."

8. In what way did the ancient Greeks use the word "motion" differently from our ordinary usage?

   The ancient Greeks used the word "motion" to describe any kind of change whatsoever whereas when we say "motion" we are only referring to change in location or place.

9. What is one of the assumptions about distances that Zeno (very naturally) makes in his argument?

   One of Zeno's assumptions about distances was that distances are infinitely divisible, that they can be divided in half forever.

10. What is the difference between a genuine mathematical line and any line that we draw or imagine? How is this difference related to Plato's theory of the Forms?

    A genuine mathematical line has length but no breadth or thickness whereas lines that we draw or imagine have *some* thickness. Plato believed that there really is a perfect Line, the Form of the Line, that existed in the realm of the Forms, but the lines that we draw and imagine are just shadows or copies of this Form.

11. Why is it strange to say that mathematical lines are made out of points?

It is strange to say that mathematical lines are made out of points because points have no dimensions at all, not even length. It seems incoherent to say that a line which has length is entirely made up of points which have no length.

12. Are lines of different lengths made up of different numbers of points? Explain.

    Lines of different lengths are not made up of different numbers of points. Every line, no matter how long or short, is made up of an infinite number of points.

13. What does "continuous" mean when we're talking about lines?

    When we call a line continuous, we mean that it has no gaps, that there are no empty places along the line.

14. Explain why no point is immediately next to any other point on a line.

    If you choose two points which are as close as you can possibly imagine, then because the line has no gaps, we can zoom in on those two points and find another point in between them. We can do this for any two points, no matter how close they are, so no point can be immediately next to another point.

15. What are the fundamental or most basic entities/objects of geometry?

    The most basic entities of geometry are points and lines.

16. What part of mathematics can be called the "science of space"?

    Geometry can be called "the science of space."

17. How are mathematical lines and physical distance in space different? How are they alike? Why are their similarities important?

    Mathematical lines and physical distance in space are different because mathematical lines are mathematical objects, not physical ones, whereas physical distance is physical. We take the similarity between mathematical lines and physical distance for granted, so much so that we do not question when a line is used to represent distance. The similarity between Mathematical lines and physical distance is important because it allows us to use mathematics in science.

18. Give some examples of mathematical objects from geometry. Give some examples of physical objects. Is a square a physical or a mathematical object?

Rectangles and circles are mathematical objects from geometry. A piece of paper and a plate are physical objects. A perfect square is a mathematical object, in part because it is made up of mathematical lines which can neither be truly drawn or imagined.

19. How is the similarity between mathematical objects and the physical world a "double-edged sword"?

    The similarity between mathematical objects and the physical world is a "double-edged" sword because on the one hand, without this similarity, we couldn't use mathematics in science and therefore couldn't do science as we know it. On the other hand, this similarity poses real-life problems for anyone who takes up Plato's Pythagorean challenge, including scientists who need mathematics to describe some aspect of nature.

20. Why is Plato's challenge also called "Plato's *Pythagorean challenge*"?

    Plato's challenge is also called "Plato's Pythagorean challenge" because the Pythagoreans believed that "all is number" and Plato's challenge is basically trying to prove that statement true.

21. What two realms does the number line unite?

    The number line unites the realm of numbers and the realm of points.

22. What do we mean by "numerical address" in the case of the number line?

    By "numerical address" we mean that every point on a number line is paired with its own personal number.

23. Why can we say that 1.5 is *between* 1 and 2?

    We can say that 1.5 is *between* 1 and 2 because when we place 1 and 2 on the number line, the point which corresponds to 1.5 is located between the points which correspond to 1 and 2.

24. Why is no number immediately next to any other number?

    No number is immediately next to any other number because, like we discovered with points on the number line, if you choose two numbers which are very close together, there will always be room for a third number in between

the two original numbers. This can be done for any two numbers no matter how close together they are.

25. Numbers and lines share the strangeness of what two important (and related) concepts?

    Numbers and lines share the strangeness associated with continuity and infinity.

26. In what way can we "see" numbers?

    We can "see" numbers when we place them on a number line. For example, we can easily see that 2 is greater than 1 on a number line because 2 appears to the right of 1.

27. Draw the triangle diagram that shows the relation between numbers, shapes, (lines and points), and space. Can you explain it to someone who hasn't read about this? Why are these relations crucial for science?

    See figure 2.5.
    These relationships are crucial for science because the similarity between physical space and numbers allows us to quantify physical things, we can talk about the physical world by talking about numbers. Because of this, we can discover important truths about the world by calculating numbers.

28. How can the behavior of numbers tell us about the behavior of the physical world? Can you give specific examples? (We haven't yet covered examples in this book, so you'll have to pull from previous classes.)

    The behavior of numbers can tell us about the behavior of the physical world when numbers stand in for physical objects, kind of like stunt doubles for those physical objects. A car travelling at 60 miles per hour will arrive at its destination 10 miles away in 10 minutes. (Examples will vary.)

29. We often represent time spatially. Explain and give two examples (the examples from the book).

    We often refer to time with spatial metaphors like *in* time. You can be *in* a classroom, but what does it mean to be *in* time? We can represent time spatially on a timeline using dates to see the *distance* (another spatial metaphor)

between different historical events or figures. We can also represent time on a mathematical line in physics where different intervals of time like seconds are represented by points on the line.

30. Draw the updated version of the "similar structure" triangle.

    See figure 2.7.

31. The similarities between the structures of mathematics and those of the physical universe can cause real headaches. But there are more positive than negative implications. How might these positive implications provide evidence for a divine designer?

    The positive implications of the similarities between the structures of mathematics and the physical universe provide evidence for a designer because there is no reason for us to expect that the universe would be such a user-friendly place. The world could have been much more difficult to figure out—impossible, in fact. The best explanation for this user-friendliness is that there's someone who wants us to know about His creation, that there is a divine designer.

CHAPTER 3 - THE PARADOX OF SPEED

ANSWERS TO THE STUDY QUESTIONS

1. Do you think that mathematics is invented, discovered, or both? Why? (I haven't given you the answer to this; you're on your own.)

   The world is a mathematical place, take for example the ratios that the Pythagoreans noticed in music. So mathematics is discovered. At the same time mathematics is expressed in a language invented by humans and different expressions of the mathematics can lead to new discoveries, take for example the Cartesian coordinate system. So in a way, mathematics is partly invented as well.

2. What's the main, overall problem from Western science and philosophy that we're trying to tackle?

   The main, overall problem from Western science and philosophy that we're trying to tackle is the problem of change.

3. What is the specific problem we're dealing with in this chapter? (Just give the name at this point.)

   The specific problem we're dealing in this chapter is the problem of speed or velocity.

4. Roughly speaking, during what century did the Scientific Revolution occur? What was this revolution the birth of? What was the culmination of this revolution?

   The Scientific Revolution occurred in the 1600s. The Scientific Revolution led to the development of modern science. The culmination of the revolution is calculus.

5. The concept of speed is the combination of two other concepts we've considered. What are these two concepts?

The two concepts that we combine to form our concept of speed are space and time.

6. In symbols, what is our ordinary concept of speed or velocity? (Remember we'll be using 'speed' and 'velocity' as synonyms, which isn't exactly correct.)

$$v = \frac{d}{t}$$

7. In words (not equations), what is the difference between average speed and instantaneous speed?

   Average speed refers to the speed you were traveling over an interval of time. Instantaneous speed refers to how fast you are going at any given moment or instant.

8. Average speed is not usually the same as actual speed; but sometimes it could be. Explain.

   If you were to travel at a constant speed of 50 mph, then your average speed over an interval of time would be 50 mph and at any moment that you were travelling you were also travelling at 50 mph. In this case, the average speed and the actual speed, the instantaneous speed, would be the same.

9. Why might someone say that average speed doesn't really exist?

   Someone might say that average speed doesn't really exist because it does not describe the speed that you were travelling at any given moment, that is, average speed might not tell us what was actually happening.

10. What is the difference between a line-segment and a point?

    The difference between a line-segment and a point is that a line segment has at least some length, whereas a point has no dimension at all.

11. How is the word "instant" related to a point?

    We can represent an interval of time with a line-segment. An instant in time could be represented by a point on the line. But just as points in a line have no dimension, so too a point in time or an instant in time takes up no space on the

timeline. Also, there are an infinite number of instants in any given interval just as there are an infinite number of points in any given line-segment.

12. What is the difference between an instant and an interval of time?

    An instant of time takes up no space on a timeline, whereas an interval of time does take up space on a timeline.

13. What is a "moment"?

    A "moment" is an instant of time.

14. In words, what does "Δ" mean?

    Δ means "change in."

15. In terms of variables, what is "Δ*t*" shorthand for?

    Δ*t* is shorthand for "change in time."

16. As a formula, what is an *instant* of time in terms of "Δ*t*"? What is an *interval* of time in terms of time in terms of "Δ*t*"?

    In an instant of time, $\Delta t = 0$. In an interval of time, $\Delta t > 0$.

17. In terms of variables, what does "Δ*x*" mean? Although could have stood for anything, it stood for a physical property in our example. What physical property was that?

    Δ*x* means "change in location." The physical property that *x* stood for is location.

18. If my change in location, "Δ*x*", (that is, my distance traveled) is 100 miles, what are x_f and x_i? Answer: we don't know really. So, then, why did we choose $x_i = 0$?

    If my change in location is 100 miles, then x_f = 100 miles and x_i = 0 miles. We chose x_i = 0 miles because we don't have a standard numerical designation for individual locations like we do with time. In other words, we can call a certain point in time 2:00PM but we do not have a standard numerical designation for an individual location.

19. Why might we say that the symbol "Δ" represents what calculus is all about?

We might say that the symbol "Δ" represents what calculus is all about because that symbol means "change in." Since calculus is about solving the problem of change, the symbol which means "change in" carries a lot of meaning.

20. We could ask the previous question a bit differently: What is calculus?

    Calculus is the mathematics of change.

21. Why are we using "v" to stand for speed?

    We are using "v" to stand for speed because "v" means "velocity" and we are using "velocity" and "speed" interchangeably in this book.

22. In terms of "Δ" what did d stand for?

    In terms of "Δ", stands for a very, very small, an infinitesimally small change in something.

23. In terms of "Δ" what is v_{ave}? What is v_{ave} in terms of t_f, t_i, etc.?

    In terms of "Δ", $v_{ave} = \frac{\Delta x}{\Delta t}$. In terms of t_f, t_i, and x_f, x_i, $v_{ave} = \frac{x_f - x_i}{t_f - t_i}$

24. What is the paradox of speed? Make sure to express it in words as well as in Δ notation.

    The paradox of speed is that instantaneous speed doesn't seem to make any sense. When we consider an object changing location, it seems that it is moving at every moment in time, at every instant. However, in an instant of time, no time passes, and if no time passes, then no distance can be travelled. The paradox is that in any given instant, no motion occurs, but this does not fit with our observations. We can express this in Δ notation this way: $v_{ave} = \frac{\Delta x}{\Delta t} = \frac{0}{0}$. Here we see another problem. We have a zero in the denominator which is undefined or meaningless.

CHAPTER 4 - THE PLATONIC-PYTHAGOREAN PROJECT BEFORE THE SCIENTIFIC REVOLUTION

ANSWERS TO THE STUDY QUESTIONS

1. What is the "Platonic-Pythagorean project"?

   The Platonic-Pythagorean project is the general project of uncovering the mathematical order of nature that hides behind the chaotic appearances.

2. What do I say is your main goal here with respect to calculus?

   The main goal is to understand the core fundamentals of calculus.

3. Who gave the problem of change a mathematical twist?

   Pythagoras and Plato gave the problem of change a mathematical twist.

4. What is one of the main goals of science?

   One of the main goals of science is to understand change in mathematical terms.

5. What do we mean by "quantifying" motion?

   "Quantifying" motion means attaching numbers to it. In other words, quantifying motion is describing motion using numbers.

6. What were two main difficulties with the project of describing nature mathematically? For the "second" difficulty, make sure you can name the concepts that give rise to the difficulties.

   One difficulty with describing nature mathematically is that it is just plain hard. Not all physical phenomena can be described as simply as music with its whole number ratios. The other difficulty with describing nature mathematically is that we encounter problems with change, in our specific case, problems with change in location. Space, time, and numbers, the three concepts which we use to describe change in location, all have their own problems which arise from the concepts of continuity and infinity.

7. What are the difficulties specifically related to speed?

   The difficulties specifically related to speed come from the difficulties we encounter when dealing with space, time, and number. For instance, the very concept of instantaneous speed seems incoherent when we recognize that no distance can be travelled in an instant. And yet, when we observe an object in motion, it seems that it is moving at each instant, not standing still.

8. What is Plato's "Pythagoras-inspired" project?

   Plato's Pythagoras-inspired project is to mathematically describe the heavenly motions.

9. Explain how it was possible to temporarily set aside the conceptual problems associated with motion. Why was the Pythagorean problem—when it came to the heavens—still difficult?

   It was possible to temporarily set aside the conceptual problems associated with motion because the planets did not appear to have any motion in an instant. Philosophers could think of Plato's project in terms of a series of photographs rather than as one continuous motion. But the Pythagorean problem was still difficult to solve because the heavenly bodies move in fairly complicated ways. A further difficulty for mathematicians was that they needed to describe the motion of the heavenly bodies using spheres, even though the motion of the planets wasn't circular.

10. Who was the first to answer Plato's challenge? What geometrical (i.e., mathematical) shape did he use? How many of these did it take to describe the motion of Mercury?

    Eudoxus, Plato's student, was the first to answer Plato's challenge. He solved the problem using spheres. It took four spheres rotating about one another to describe the motion of Mercury.

11. How many spheres did Eudoxus use for the entire cosmos? Was his system exact?

    Eudoxus used twenty-seven spheres to describe the motion of all the heavenly bodies. His system was not exact but it came closer than it had a right to.

12. Did Plato and Eudoxus actually believe that the spheres existed and were causing the motion of the planets? What is the important distinction related to this; that is, *cause* as opposed to what?

    Plato and Eudoxus did not believe that the spheres actually existed or that the spheres were the true cause the motion of the planets, instead they were merely interested in mapping the motion of the celestial objects. The distinction related to this is the distinction between simply describing motion and determining the cause for motion. Plato and Eudoxus were not concerned with the cause of the motion of the planets, they just wanted to accurately describe it.

13. The sign above the entrance to Plato's Academy said, "Let no one ignorant of *geometry* enter here" and not "Let no one ignorant of *mathematics* enter here." Why?

    The sign above Plato's Academy used the word *geometry* instead of *mathematics* because, for the Greeks, geometry was the main discipline of mathematics.

14. What is Euclid's *Elements*? Why is it so important? What is so surprising about it?

    Euclid's *Elements* is the canon of ancient Greek mathematics. What is so surprising about Euclid's *Elements* is that contains no numbers, only theorems and proofs about shapes.

15. Why is the distinction between celestial and terrestrial objects important for the problem of change?

    The distinction between celestial and terrestrial objects is important for the problem of change because it was significantly easier to use mathematics to describe the motion of celestial objects than it was to mathematically describe the motion of earthly objects.

16. How did Aristotle differ from Plato regarding Forms?

    Aristotle, unlike Plato, denied that there was a world of the Forms. He believed that the forms existed, but instead of saying that the forms existed in their own realm, he said that the forms were present within individual ordinary objects here in our physical universe.

17. What was science called for most of Western history?

    For most of Western history, *science* was called *natural philosophy*.

18. Did Aristotle think that mathematics was important? Explain.

    Aristotle thought that mathematics was important; he thought it was the most secure kind of knowledge we can have.

19. Aristotle's view of the Forms made the problem of change a bit more difficult to solve mathematically. How so?

    Aristotle's view of the forms made the problem of change more difficult to solve mathematically because he believed the forms were actually in the terrestrial objects and those objects are more difficult to describe mathematically.

20. Was Aristotle interested in Plato's project? Explain.

    Aristotle was interested in Plato's project. He and his students even modified Eudoxus's celestial system of spheres, making it more accurate as well as more complicated, increasing the number of spheres to more than fifty.

21. An answer to a previous question was the distinction between descriptions and causes. How was this distinction related to the difference between Plato and Aristotle's goal of science or natural philosophy?

    Plato believed that describing or mapping the motion of the planets, describing the world mathematically, was the main goal of natural philosophy. Aristotle on the other hand believed that the primary goal of natural philosophy was to discover what *causes* objects to move the way they do, not merely to describe their motion.

22. What were the celestial spheres made of, according to Aristotle?

    Aristotle believed that the celestial spheres were transparent crystalline spheres composed of ether or quintessence.

23. What did the ancient Greeks (including Aristotle) think composed terrestrial objects?

    The ancient Greeks believed that terrestrial objects were composed of four elements: earth, air, fire, and water.

24. Was Aristotle's system of spheres a mathematical or physical system?

    Aristotle's system of spheres was a mathematical system, but it was nearly the extent of his mathematical attack on the problem of change, and unlike Plato it wasn't merely mathematical, it was also physical.

25. What are the four causes and why are they important?

    Aristotle's four causes are the material, efficient, formal, and final causes. They are important because they were Aristotle's solution to the problem of change, and the Scientific Revolution was an overthrowing of Aristotle's largely non-mathematical science.

26. What do *we* say causes a dropped ball to fall? What does Aristotle say the cause is? In each case, *where* are these causes?

    We say that gravity causes a dropped ball to fall. Aristotle says that the ball's nature causes it to fall. Gravity is an external cause whereas Aristotle's answer made the cause internal.

27. What is a "nature" according to Aristotle? How does an object's nature cause it to fall?

    According to Aristotle, an object's nature is dictated by its composition (earth, air, fire, or water). Terrestrial objects that are composed of earth find their natural resting place at the center of the earth, whereas objects composed of fire find their natural resting place just inside the moon's orbit.

28. According to Aristotle, what causes fire to rise?

    According to Aristotle, fire rises because the natural resting place of fire is just inside the moon's orbit and the fire is tending towards that natural resting place.

29. What does the Greek word *physis* mean? What word do we derive from it?

    The Greek word *physis* means *nature,* and it is the source of our word *physics.*

30. What is the "principle of change"?

    Aristotle said that the principle of change is an object's nature.

31. In your own words, what is the goal of Aristotle's physics?

The goal of Aristotle's physics is to find an objects nature and to explain why something changes.

32. The medieval Scholastics paraphrased Aristotle's goal of physics with a famous saying. What was that saying?

    The medieval Scholastics paraphrased Aristotle's goal of physics with this famous saying: "Ignorance of motion is ignorance of nature."

33. Did Aristotle think that objects like rocks were alive since they "sought" their natural place when dropped?

    Aristotle did not believe that objects like rocks were alive though he did view the cosmos more like a giant organism than like a giant clock as we often do.

34. Why did Aristotle state his law of free fall with only words (and not with mathematical symbols)?

    Aristotle stated his law of free fall with only words and not with mathematical symbols because, prior to Descartes's invention of algebraic notation, mathematics was done with ordinary words.

35. From memory, draw and label the diagram of the two free falling balls from figure 4.8.

    See figure 4.8.

36. What is Aristotle's law of free fall in terms of a formula (without the delta notation)?

$$\frac{w_1}{w_2} = \frac{d_1}{t_1} \cdot \frac{t_2}{d_2}$$

37. Write Aristotle's law of free fall using the delta notation.

$$\frac{w_1}{w_2} = \frac{\Delta h_1}{\Delta t_1} \cdot \frac{t_2}{\Delta h_2}$$

38. Aristotle's law of fall is actually false. What do you think is wrong with it?

    I think that the problem with Aristotle's law of fall is that, while it is true that heavier things fall faster than lighter things (think of a bowling ball and

a feather) nevertheless the reason the heavier thing falls faster is because it can cut through the air faster.

39. Does Aristotle's law of free fall say what causes objects to fall? Explain.

    Aristotle's law of free fall does not say what causes objects to fall, it simply describes their falling behavior.

40. What is the discipline that studies forces acting on stationary objects?

    The discipline that studies forces acting on stationary objects is called *statics*.

41. When did Archimedes die? When did Aristotle die?

    Archimedes died in 212 BC. Aristotle died in 323 BC.

42. What does "*Eureka*" mean?

    "Eureka" means "I found it."

43. What does it mean to say that a lever is in equilibrium?

    To say that a lever is in equilibrium is to say that the forces acting on the lever cancel each other out or that the lever is balanced.

44. Write out, in words, Archimedes' Law of the Lever. Draw a diagram for this but without labeling.

    Archimedes' law of the Lever is this: "Two magnitudes balance at distances reciprocally proportional to the magnitudes."

    See figure 4.9b.

45. Label the Law of the Lever diagram and write it out as a formula.

    See figure 4.9b and the formulas on page 66.

46. How might a lever be an analogy for an equation?

    A lever can be an analogy for an equation because like an equation, a lever in equilibrium is balanced. Also, just like equations, whatever you do to one side of the lever, you must do the same to the other side to keep it balanced.

47. What is Archimedes's Principle?

Archimedes's Principle is that "Any solid lighter than a fluid will, if placed in the fluid, be so far immersed that the weight of the solid will be equal to the weight of the fluid displaced."

48. Draw a diagram showing how Archimedes's Principle can be thought of as a lever problem.

    See figure 4.9e.

49. What is hydrostatics?

    Hydrostatics is the discipline that studies forces acting on stationary objects in water or some other fluid.

50. How was Archimedes's work a step forward in mankind's work on the problem of change?

    Archimedes's work was a step forward in mankind's work on the problem of change because he successfully applied mathematics to a number of important terrestrial phenomena.

51. Who wrote the *Almagest*? When did he die? What does "*Almagest*" mean?

    Claudius Ptolemy wrote the *Almagest*. He died in AD 168. "*Almagest*" means "the greatest."

52. What does "trigonometry" mean?

    "Trigonometry" means "the measurement of triangles."

53. What is Scholasticism?

    Scholasticism is the combination of Aristotle with Christianity.

54. Why were Scholastic philosophers and theologians so impressed with Aristotle?

    The Scholastic philosophers were so impressed with Aristotle because his work in physics, metaphysics, logic, politics, aesthetics, ethics, and biology were so comprehensive, elaborate, and internally consistent.

55. Why didn't Plato's Pythagorean approach to science advance very much between Aristotle and the time of the Scholastics?

Plato's Pythagorean approach to science didn't advance very much between Aristotle and the time of the Scholastics in part due to the difficulty of applying mathematics to the physical world.

56. Who will eventually replace Aristotle as the ruler of science after the Scientific Revolution?

    Newton will eventually replace Aristotle as the ruler of science after the Scientific Revolution.

EXERCISE SOLUTIONS

1) $\frac{w_1}{w_2} = \frac{v_1}{v_2} \Rightarrow \frac{100}{10} = \frac{v_1}{v_2} \Rightarrow 10 = \frac{v_1}{v_2} \Rightarrow v_1 = 10v_2$

2) $\frac{w_m}{w_b} = \frac{d_b}{d_m} \Rightarrow d_m = \frac{d_b \cdot w_b}{w_m} = 10 \text{ ft} \cdot \frac{500 \text{ lb}}{200 \text{ lb}} = 10 \text{ ft} \cdot \frac{5}{2} = 25 \text{ ft}$

CHAPTER 5 - THE SCIENTIFIC REVOLUTION AND THE NEED FOR CALCULUS

ANSWERS TO THE STUDY QUESTIONS

1. The Scientific Revolution occurred mostly in which century? What are two more specific dates that are helpful bookends to the Scientific Revolution?

   The Scientific Revolution occurred mostly in the 1600's or the 17th century. Two specific dates that are helpful bookends to the Scientific revolution are 1543, the year that Nicolaus Copernicus's *On the Revolution of the Heavenly Spheres* was published, and 1727, the year Isaac Newton died

2. What are the years of Galileo's birth and death?

   Galileo was born in 1564 and died in 1642.

3. What is this chapter about?

   This chapter gives a brief overview of some important developments leading up to calculus and it shows further why calculus was needed. In particular, this chapter focuses on Galileo Galilei's role in ending Aristotle's two-thousand year reign.

4. Why is the Scientific Revolution called a "revolution"? Why is it called a "scientific" revolution?

   The Scientific Revolution is called a "revolution" because it overthrew the existing regime. It is called a "scientific" revolution because it overthrew the *scientific* regime of Aristotle.

5. What was so impressive about Aristotle's philosophy? Why did this make modifying it difficult? What did this have to do with Christianity?

   Aristotle's philosophy was so impressive because it was a comprehensive and coherent system that touched on nearly everything from logic to physics to astronomy to biology to ethics to politics. It was also impressive because all these things were intricately woven together. This made modifying the system

difficult because to challenge one tenet of the philosophy would change other things as well. Because Aristotle's philosophy was alloyed with Christianity in what was often called Scholasticisim, an attack on Aristotle's philosophy could be perceived as an attack on Christianity.

6. What is the main achievement of the Scientific Revolution?

   The main achievement of the Scientific Revolution is the mathematization of motion, the fulfillment of the Platonic-Pythagorean dream.

7. What is calculus?

   Calculus is the mathematics of change.

8. How might we characterize the Scientific Revolution in terms of the Platonic-Pythagorean tradition?

   We might say as the eminent historian of science Richard Westfall did that the Scientific Revolution was dominated or characterized by the resurgence of the "Platonic-Pythagorean tradition, which looked on nature in geometric terms, convinced that the cosmos was constructed according to the principles of mathematical order.

9. Whom does Heisenberg say that modern physics favors?

   Heisenberg says that modern physics favors Plato.

10. In summary, what are the three main results of the Scientific Revolution? What is a fourth?

    The three main results of the Scientific Revolution are: first, the overthrow of Aristotle; second, the reintroduction of the Platonic-Pythagorean project; and third, the mathematization of motion. A fourth result of the Scientific Revolution is the development of the mechanical philosophy, the philosophy that views the universe like a machine (e.g. a clock) as opposed to Aristotle's philosophy which viewed the world more like a living organism.

11. Why was Copernicus important? When did he die?

Copernicus was important because he fired the first shot of the Scientific Revolution. He proposed a sun-centered (*heliocentric*) universe in favor of the earth-centered (geocentric) universe. Copernicus died in 1543.

12. What is heliocentricity? What is geocentricity?

    Heliocentricity is the idea that the sun is at the center of the universe. Geocentricity is the idea that the earth is at the center of the universe.

13. What was another name for "heliocentricity" during the Scientific Revolution?

    During the Scientific Revolution, "Pythagoreanism" was another name for "heliocentricity."

14. What was the name of Copernicus's famous book? What does the word "revolution" refer to in the title?

    The name of Copernicus's famous book was *On the Revolutions of the Heavenly Spheres*. The word "revolution" in the title refers to the motion of the heavenly bodies (e.g. the earth revolves around the sun).

15. What was the appeal of heliocentricity for Copernicus?

    The appeal of heliocentricity for Copernicus was that it made the mathematical description of the heavens—and therefore calculations of the church calendar—easier.

16. Why did the Roman Catholic Church initially ignore Copernicus's book?

    The Roman Catholic Church initially ignored Copernicus' book because most people considered the heliocentric view merely as a mathematical device for calculating the dates of astronomical events; they didn't really believe that Copernicus was suggesting an actual physical theory of the earth literally revolving around the sun.

17. Why did Kepler think that Copernicus's system ought to be simplified? What year did Kepler die?

    Kepler thought that Copernicus's system needed to be simplified because it was a complex system, requiring a large number of circles, including epicycles.

Kepler found the key to this simplicity by modeling the orbits of the planets as ellipses rather than perfect circles. Kepler died in 1630.

18. Why was heliocentricity dangerous for all of Aristotelianism and not just for its geocentricity?

    Heliocentricity was dangerous for all of Aristotelianism and not just for its geocentricity because Aristotle's system was internally consistent and to change one thing meant other things would have to change as well. For example, to take the earth out of the center of the universe meant that the behavior of falling objects could no longer be explained by their earthy nature, their tendency to seek the center of the universe.

19. What is cosmology? What is the difference between cosmology and terrestrial physics?

    Cosmology is the study of the overall structure of the cosmos. The difference between cosmology and terrestrial physics is that cosmology deals with the whole cosmos whereas terrestrial physics deals with the physics on earth. So terrestrial physics deals with cannonballs while it does not deal with the motion of Venus.

20. Why is this chapter discussing the terrestrial physics of Galileo?

    This chapter is discussing the terrestrial physics of Galileo because, in the wake of heliocentrism toppling geocentrism, Galileo realized that an entirely new physics was needed.

21. What book got Galileo interested in mathematics?

    The book that got Galileo interested in mathematics was Euclid's *Elements.*

22. How did Archimedes influence Galileo?

    Archimedes's mathematical statics and hydrostatics, which proceeded in the same axiomatic form as Euclid's *Elements,* were the foundation on which Galileo built his own work.

23. What two kinds of motion did Galileo mainly focus on?

    Galileo mainly focused on the motion of falling objects and projectiles.

24. Why did Galileo use inclined planes to study the motion of falling objects? What other apparatus did he use to study free fall?

    Galileo used inclined planes to study the motion of falling objects because objects fall quickly and measuring the time it takes for them to fall is difficult. He used inclined plains to slow things down. Galileo also used pendulums to perform free fall experiments.

25. In addition to how fast objects fall, what was another difficulty with the speed of such objects?

    Another difficulty with measuring the speed of falling objects is that their velocity isn't constant—it changes continuously.

26. What was Galileo's "new science"? What made it new?

    Galileo's "new science" was the science of motion. What made it new was its methods: the use of mathematics and experiments.

27. Describe in your own words Galileo's view about mathematics and the "book of nature."

    Galileo believed that the "book of nature," the universe, was written in the language of mathematics and that a person ignorant of the language of mathematics could not understand what was set before him in nature.

28. Galileo discovered his law of free fall using experiments. What is the mathematical form of this law?

$$\frac{d_1}{t_1^2} = \frac{d_2}{t_2^2}$$

29. Write Galileo's law of free fall in the version that doesn't rely on the ratio of two separate events (but refers to the acceleration constant).

$$d = \frac{1}{2}at^2$$

30. The units of acceleration, ft/s^2, seems strange (what's a second squared, after all?). Explain these units in a way that makes more sense.

ft/s² means ft/s per second. So the unit ft/s² tells us how much an objects speed (expressed in ft/s) changes over time, hence the second "s" in the denominator.

31. For this version of Galileo's law of free fall,

$$d = 16t^2$$

What are the units of measurement for d and t?

For this version of Galileo's law of free fall, d is measured in feet and t is measured in seconds.

32. Why can't we calculate the speed of an object at the final moment of its fall using Galileo's law of free fall?

Galileo's law of free fall only tells us the average speed of a falling object over its entire fall, it does not tell us the falling object's instantaneous speed.

EXERCISE SOLUTIONS

1) $d = v_{ave} \cdot t \Rightarrow v_{ave} = \frac{d}{t} \Rightarrow \frac{d_1}{d_2} = \frac{w_1}{w_2} \cdot \frac{t_1}{t_2} \Rightarrow \frac{d_1}{t_1} \cdot \frac{t_2}{d_2} = \frac{w_1}{w_2}$

$\Rightarrow v_{ave,1} \cdot \frac{1}{v_{ave,2}} = \frac{w_1}{w_2} \Rightarrow \frac{v_{ave,1}}{v_{ave,2}} = \frac{w_1}{w_2}$

2) $d = v_{ave} \cdot t \Rightarrow v_{ave} = \frac{d}{t} \Rightarrow \frac{d_1}{d_2} = \frac{t_1^2}{t_2^2} = \frac{t_1 \cdot t_1}{t_2 \cdot t_2} \Rightarrow \frac{d_1}{t_1} \cdot \frac{t_2}{d_2} = \frac{t_1}{t_2}$

$\Rightarrow v_{ave,1} \cdot \frac{1}{v_{ave,2}} = \frac{t_1}{t_2} \Rightarrow \frac{v_{ave,1}}{v_{ave,2}} = \frac{t_1}{t_2}$

3) $d = 16t^2 = 16 \cdot (3)^2 = 16 \cdot 9 = 144$ ft

CHAPTER 6 - NEWTON AND CALCULUS

ANSWERS TO THE STUDY QUESTIONS

1. What are the three main characteristics of the Scientific Revolution?

   The three main characteristics of the Scientific Revolution are:
   1. **The overthrow of Aristotle.**
   2. **The reintroduction of the Platonic-Pythagorean project.**
   3. **The mathematization of motion.**

2. What was Galileo's view on cosmology?

   Galileo had a Copernican or heliocentric view of cosmology.

3. What was one of Galileo's views on terrestrial physics?

   One of Galileo's views on terrestrial physics has to do with his law of free fall. Galileo discovered a way of mathematically describing falling objects.

4. In addition to mathematics, what else did Newton study?

   In addition to mathematics, Newton also studied optics, chemistry, and theology.

5. What did Aristotle say is the cause of change?

   Aristotle said that the cause of change was to be found in an object's nature. For example, a rock would fall to the earth because its essence was earthy and so it would tend to its natural place of rest, that is, the center of the earth.

6. What did people think the celestial realm was made of? What about the terrestrial realm? Why did this pose a problem for a unified physics of the cosmos?

   People thought that the celestial realm was made of a fifth essence called *aether.* They thought that the terrestrial realm was composed of four elements—earth, air, fire, and water. This posed a problem for a unified physics of the cosmos because it required to different sets of laws—laws that governed the terrestrial realm and laws that governed the celestial realm.

7. What is another name for the terrestrial realm? Why is it called this?

   Another name for the terrestrial realm is the sublunary realm.

8. What is another name for aether?

   Another name for aether is quintessence.

9. If Copernican cosmology (heliocentricity) were true it would require scientists—natural philosophers—to develop an entirely new terrestrial physics, which would be an extremely difficult task. Yet why was this also a good thing?

   The overthrow of the Aristotelian cosmology would mean that scientists would have to develop a new terrestrial physics, which would be a difficult task, but this was also a good thing because it would mean that only a single set of laws would be needed to describe the entire cosmos.

10. What is the full name of Newton's *Principia* (in English?) In what year was it first published? How is unifying physics related to Newton's *Principia*? How is this related to the problem of change and calculus?

    The full English name of Newton's *Principia* is *The Mathematical Principles of Natural Philosophy*. It was first published in 1687. In his work, Newton derived a set of mathematical laws that applied to the entire cosmos, in other words, he derived a set of mathematical laws that unified physics. The mathematical principles required calculus and were a major leap in solving the mathematized problem of change set by the Pythagoreans and Plato.

11. Who else invented calculus, independently of Newton? Why isn't he considered as important as Newton when it comes to calculus.

    Gottfried Leibniz invented calculus independently of Newton. He isn't considered as important as Newton when it comes to calculus because, unlike Newton, Leibniz did not use his calculus to create a new physics, that is, he did not apply it to the physical world.

12. Why did Newton's *Principia* incite fervor and hope? What did this have to do with rationality or reason?

Newton's *Principia* incited fervor and hope because it uncovered the workings of the universe. Newton's *Principia* showed the power of man's reason: man's reason could plumb the depths of the cosmos, man's reason could discern the divine design and hidden truth.

13. How did Newton see his physics as religious?

    Newton saw his physics as religious because he saw his work as a way of investigating God's handiwork—indeed as a way of worshiping the God of Abraham, Isaac, and Jacob.

14. What is the Enlightenment and how did Newton's *Principia* give rise to it? Do you think Newton would have been happy with this result?

    The Enlightenment was a period in Western history when folks saw a chance to turn from religion to reason, from benighted tradition to enlightened self-dependence. I do not think that Newton would be pleased with people using science and reason to turn from God since Newton himself was a devout Christian.

15. What do some people think is the lesson of the Scientific Revolution? Why is this ironic?

    Some people think the lesson of the Scientific Revolution is that science and reason can free us from religious ignorance and oppression. This is ironic because the Scientific Revolution culminated with a Christian mathematician and scientist inventing calculus and applying it to the physical world.

16. What are the three Pythagorean theses that Morris Kline said were the core beliefs underlying the Scientific Revolution?

    The three Pythagorean theses that Morris Kline said were the core beliefs underlying the Scientific Revolution are:

    1. **The universe is ordered according to perfect mathematical laws.**
    2. **Divine reason is the orderer.**
    3. **Human reason can discern the divine mathematical pattern.**

17. Very briefly—in a single sentence—what is calculus?

    Calculus is the mathematics of change.

18. What were the four main problems that calculus was invented to solve?

    The four main problems that calculus was invented to solve were:

    1. **Describing continually changing velocity and acceleration.**
    2. **Finding the slope of a curve (including minimum and maximum values).**
    3. **Finding the tangent line to a curve.**
    4. **Finding the area under a curve.**

19. How was the way Newton imagined a mathematical curve related to the problem of change?

    Newton imagined mathematical curves on a graph as the paths of moving points, as if a point were drawing the curve as it moved. Instead of viewing the purely mathematical problem as a stationary curve, he viewed it as a point in motion so that the mathematical problem itself was a problem of motion or change.

20. Why is calculus called "calculus"? Who is responsible for this name?

    Calculus is called "calculus" because the term means "pebble" or "stone" in Latin and the Pythagoreans, for example, used pebbles to represent numbers. Leibniz picked up on this and was the first to use the term *calculus* in reference to this new mathematical tool.

21. Have we been doing mathematics in this chapter?

    We have been doing mathematics in this chapter. Solving problems is a part of mathematics but tackling mathematical problems without discussing "why" reduces mathematics to mere puzzle solving. In this and previous chapters we have been discussing the "whys" of calculus which is itself mathematics.

CHAPTER 7 - THE ESSENTIAL TOOLS: VARIABLES, FUNCTIONS, AND GRAPHS

ANSWERS TO THE STUDY QUESTIONS

1. What is a variable's job?

   A variable's job is to stand for or represent things that change.

2. Translate the formula $d=16t^2$ into an English sentence.

   The distance that a dropped object falls is equal to sixteen multiplied by the square of the time it takes to fall.

3. What, most directly, do the variables d and t represent in $d=16t^2$? Does this mean that d and t don't stand for distance and time? Explain.

   The variables d and t most directly represent numbers. However, while d and t represent numbers, they also stand for distance and time, because the numbers that they represent are themselves representations of distance and time.

4. How can the sentence, $d=16t^2$, be about both numbers and the physical properties of distance and time? How is this a Platonic and Pythagorean idea?

   The sentence, $d=16t^2$, can be about numbers and physical properties of distance and time because there is a close connection between mathematical objects (numbers) and physical ones (distances and times). It's this connection between numbers and the physical world that gave the Pythagoreans and Plato the idea that the cosmos is fundamentally mathematical in the first place.

5. How does the fact that the sentence, $d=16t^2$, being about both numbers and the physical properties, bring up our discussion of the correlation between points and numbers?

   The fact that the sentence, $d=16t^2$, is about both numbers and the physical properties brings up our discussion of the correlation between points and numbers because the variables and stand for numbers and numbers can be

placed at points on a number line. This is important because the number line has a similar structure to space and time.

6. What does it mean to *quantify* a property?

   To *quantify* a property means to represent a physical property with numbers.

7. What kinds of things can we quantify? What kinds of things don't seem to be quantifiable?

   We can quantify things like space, time, mass, velocity, acceleration, density, force, area, and volume. We can't seem to quantify things like color, pain, beauty, love, hunger, thirst, good, and evil.

8. How is *interpretation* important to mathematics? How is this like interpreting any language?

   Interpretation is important to mathematics because the mathematical symbols need to have meanings attached to them (i.e., interpreted) to convey anything meaningful. This is like interpreting any language because unless there is meaning attached to the symbols of a language, unless there is meaning attached to the individual written words, the symbols taken together are meaningless.

9. How does mathematics *predict*? Give a specific example.

   Mathematics predicts by giving us the tools to see how quantities of physical objects will change without actually dealing with the physical objects themselves. Even simple addition is an act of predicting. If you had 34 nickels and 27 quarters, you could determine the total quantity of coins using addition and if you did it right, you would come up with 61. If you then counted each individual coin, you would observe that there are in fact 61 coins. When you added, you did not deal with the physical objects themselves, instead you predicted how many there would be. When you counted the coins individually, you observed that your prediction was correct.

10. In terms of change, what is velocity? This is, what *two things* are changing?

    Velocity has to do with how much distance changes as time changes.

11. In terms of change, what is acceleration? That is, what *two things* are changing?

    Acceleration has to do with how much velocity changes as time changes.

12. What is a function?

    A function is a relation between variables.

13. Express the function that relates distance and time for a falling object. Is there more than one way to express this function? Explain.

    The function that relates distance and time for a falling object is $d=16t^2$. We can express this using the algebraic formula, as we just did, or we can use an ordinary sentence, *the distance that a dropped object falls is equal to sixteen multiplied by the square of the time it takes to fall.*

14. What is a graph and why is it useful?

    A graph is a picture of a function, it *shows* how variables behave together. It is useful because sometimes it is much easier to *see* how variables behave than to have their behavior described in words or formulas.

15. How is a Cartesian plane like a number line? How is it different?

    A Cartesian plane is like a number line on steroids. It is two number lines combined, a two-dimensional number plane. Like a number line, points on a Cartesian plane still have their own unique numerical address, but on a Cartesian plane the address is composed of two numbers.

16. What are two ways to represent a function? How are they different from each other? What are the benefits of each?

    The two ways to represent a function are as a formula or on a graph. Formulas are like efficient sentences and graphs are like pictures. The benefit of formulas is that they allow us to precisely calculate numerical values and the value of graphs is that they allow us to picture the relationship between variables.

17. What is analytic geometry?

    Analytic geometry is a mathematical system that combines algebraic formulas with pictures in Cartesian coordinates. In other words, analytic geometry is

the algebraic representation of shapes and the geometrical representation of algebraic formulas.

18. In the function represented by the formula $y=13x^2+3$ what is the dependent variable? Which is the independent variable? Why?

    In the function represented by the formula $y=13x^2+3$, the dependent variable is y and the independent variable is x. There is nothing more special about x that makes it the dependent variable, it is simply convention. Convention dictates that x is the input variable, the value that we place into the function, and the value for y will depend on that input variable, so y is the dependent variable.

    In this function, if the value of the independent variable, the value of x, were 1, then we would square it, multiply it by 13, and add 3, giving us 16. So the value of y, the dependent variable, in this case 16, depended on the value of the independent variable, the value of x, in this case 1.

19. What exactly do we mean by "independent" and "dependent"? What is depending on what? What is independent of what?

    By "independent" we mean that the value of this variable does not depend on anything else in the function. By "dependent" we mean that that value of this variable will depend on the value of the independent variable. The dependent variable depends on the independent variable. The independent variable does not depend on the dependent variable.

20. What might be the advantage of writing $d(t)=16t^2$ rather than $d=16t^2$?

    The advantage of writing $d(t)=16t^2$ is that $d(t)$ will remind us that distance is a function of time. It will remind us that the distance traveled will depend on how much time has elapsed.

21. What are the three main concepts of calculus? What law tells us that all of them are related?

    The three main concepts of calculus are:

    1. **The limit of a function**
    2. **The derivative of a function**
    3. **The integral of a function**

The law that tells us that all of these are related is the *Fundamental Theorem of Calculus*.

CHAPTER 8 - A NEW TOOL: THE LIMIT

ANSWERS TO THE STUDY QUESTIONS

1. What is the paradox of speed?

   The paradox of speed is that speed is something that is clearly physically real but that seems mathematically incoherent. Something with speed is clearly moving at any given instant, but to calculate an object's speed would require us to divide by 0 which is meaningless or undefined.

2. In this chapter are we solving the paradox of speed? If not, then what *are* we doing in this chapter?

   In this chapter we are not solving the paradox of speed. Instead, we are becoming familiar with a new mathematical tool, the limit, which we will use to solve the paradox of speed later.

3. According to our conventional notation, what is the input of the function $f(x)$? What is the output?

   According to our conventional notation, the input of the function $f(x)$ is x and the output is $f(x)$.

4. What x-value is forbidden for the following function?

$$f(x) = \frac{x^2 + x}{x}$$

   Why is the x-value forbidden?

   For the function $f(x) = \frac{x^2 + x}{x}$ the forbidden x-value is 0. 0 is the forbidden x-value because, for this function, when x=0, the denominator is 0, which is meaningless or undefined.

5. For the above function, what does the output of the function approach as the x-value approaches the forbidden value?

For the above function, as the x-value approaches the forbidden value, that is, as the x-value approaches 0, the output approaches 1.

6. The general form of a line, as you know, is $y(x)=mx+b$. Why then, can the above function $f(x)$ also be represented by a line?

   At first glance, the above function does not appear to have the general form of a line, $y(x)=mx+b$. However, we can factor out from the numerator giving us $x(x+1)$. We can then cancel out the x's in the numerator and the denominator leaving us with $f(x) = x + 1$. This derived formula now has the general form of a line where $y(x)$ is $f(x)$, m is 1, and b is 1.

7. In symbols, write the formula for the equivalent of the English sentence, "1 is the limit of the function, $f(x)$, as x approaches 0." Rewrite this formula for when

$$f(x) = \frac{x^2 + x}{x}$$

   The English sentence, "1 is the limit of the function, $f(x)$, as x approaches 0" can be rewritten in symbols this way: $\lim_{x \to 0} f(x) = 1$. When $f(x)$ $\frac{x^2 \quad x}{x}$, this formula can be rewritten as follows: $\lim_{x \to 0}\left(\frac{x^2 + x}{x}\right) = 1$.

8. In English, rewrite the formula

$$\lim_{x \to 0} f(x) = 1$$

   The formula could be written in English as, "1 is the limit of the function, $f(x)$, as x approaches 0."

9. Why did we write "$x \neq 0$" beside this formula:

$$f(x) = x + 1$$

   We wrote "$x \neq 0$" beside the formula $f(x) = x + 1$ because the formula was derived from $f(x) = \frac{x^2 + x}{x}$. In that original formula, 0 was the forbidden x-value

because it would make the denominator equal 0. So for the formula that we derived, we remember the forbidden x-value and write, "$x \neq 0$."

10. Finish the sentence, "limit = the value you approach but ______________." Why does this make the "method of substitution" somewhat misleading? Make sure you know who Tantalus is.

    "Limit = the value you approach <u>but never reach.</u>" This makes the method of substitution somewhat misleading because this method can make it look as if we're allowing our input value to equal the forbidden value when we can really only approach the forbidden value.

11. Why did we write $f(x)$ and $g(x)$ different from each other, like this:

$$f(x)=x+1 \quad x \neq 0$$
$$g(x)=x+1$$

    Even though $f(x)$ and $g(x)$ appear to be the same, we wrote the qualification for $f(x)$ that $x \neq 0$ because $f(x)$ has a history that $g(x)$ does not. $f(x) = x+1$ was derived from $f(x) \quad \frac{x^2 \quad x}{x}$ where $x \neq 0$. $g(x)$ does not have the same history and so it does not need the same qualification.

12. What is the difference between the limit of a function and the value of the function? Also, show this difference in symbols.

    The difference between the limit of a function and the value of a function is that in the first case we use *approach* and in the second case we use *equal to*. So for the formula $g(x) = x + 1$, we can say that as x approaches 0, $g(x)$ approaches 1. In this case we are talking about the limit of $g(x)$ as x approaches 0 and we can write it in symbols this way: $\lim_{x \to 0} g(x) = 1$. Or we could say that when x is equal to 0, $g(x)$ is equal to 1. In this case we are talking about the value of $g(x)$ when x is equal to 0 and we can write it in symbols this way: $g(0) = 0$.

13. Can a function have a limit and a value at the same point simultaneously?

    A function can have a limit and a value at the same point simultaneously. For example, for the formula $g(x) = x + 1$, the limit of $g(x)$ as x approaches 0 is 1. The value of $g(x)$ when x is equal to 0 is also 1.

14. For the function

$$f(x)=\frac{x^2+x}{x}$$

how close does x get to 0 when taking the limit

$$\lim_{x\to 0}\left(\frac{x^2+x}{x}\right)$$

When we take the limit of the function $f(x)=\frac{x^2+x}{x}$, x can come as close to 0 as you please, as long as it's not exactly 0. And if you want to get even closer, there is always a value closer to 0 than the one that you chose.

15. How does the metaphor of standing versus seeing help explain why limits are exact even though they are only approached but never reached?

The metaphor of standing versus seeing helps explain why limits are exact even though they are only approached but never reached because we understand that you do not need to stand on a gap to know exactly where it is. Instead, if you can get really close to the gap, you can see exactly where it is, even without standing directly on it.

EXERCISE SOLUTIONS

a. $\lim_{x\to 0}(x+2)=0+2=2$

b. $\lim_{x\to 0}(x^2+2)=0+2=2$

c. $\lim_{x\to 0}(x^2+x)=0+0=0$

d. $\frac{x^3+x}{x}=\frac{\cancel{x}(x^2+1)}{\cancel{x}}=x^2+1 \quad\Rightarrow\quad \lim_{x\to 0}\left[\frac{x^3+x}{x}\right]=\lim_{x\to 0}(x^2+1)=0+1=1$

$(x\neq 0)$

e. $\frac{x^2-9}{x-3}=\frac{(x+3)\cancel{(x-3)}}{\cancel{x-3}}=x+3 \quad\Rightarrow\quad \lim_{x\to 3}\left[\frac{x^2-9}{x-3}\right]=\lim_{x\to 3}(x+3)=6$

$(x\neq 3)$

f. $$\frac{x-4}{x^2-x-12}=\frac{\cancel{x-4}}{(\cancel{x-4})(x+3)}=\frac{1}{x+3} \Rightarrow \lim_{x\to 3}\left[\frac{x-4}{x^2-x-12}\right]$$

$$\Rightarrow \lim_{x\to 3}\left[\frac{1}{x+3}\right]=\frac{1}{6} \qquad (x\neq 4 \text{ or} -3)$$

g. $$\frac{x-4}{x^2-x-12}=\frac{\cancel{x-4}}{(\cancel{x-4})(x+3)}=\frac{1}{x+3} \Rightarrow \lim_{x\to 4}\left[\frac{x-4}{x^2-x-12}\right]$$

$$\Rightarrow \lim_{x\to 4}\left[\frac{1}{x+3}\right]=\frac{1}{7} \qquad (x\neq 4 \text{ or} -3)$$

h. $$\frac{(x-1)^2}{x-1}=\frac{(\cancel{x-1})(x-1)}{\cancel{x-1}}=x-1 \Rightarrow \lim_{x\to 1}\left[\frac{(x-1)^2}{x-1}\right]=\lim_{x\to 1}(x-1)=0$$

$(x\neq 1)$

i. $$\frac{(x+k)^2-x^2}{k}=\frac{(x+k)(x+k)-x^2}{k}=\frac{\cancel{x^2}+2kx+k^2-\cancel{x^2}}{k}=\frac{2kx+k^2}{k}$$

$$\Rightarrow \frac{\cancel{k}(2x+k)}{\cancel{k}}=2x+k \Rightarrow \lim_{k\to 0}\left[\frac{(x+k)^2-x^2}{k}\right]$$

$$\Rightarrow \lim_{k\to 0}(2x+k)=2x \qquad (k\neq 0)$$

j. $$\lim_{x\to 0}\left(\sqrt{x}\right)=0$$

k. $$\lim_{x\to 5}\left(\sqrt{5}\right)=\sqrt{5}$$

l. $$\lim_{x\to 0}\left[\frac{x^3}{x}\right]=\lim_{x\to 0}\left(x^2\right)=0 \qquad (x\neq 0)$$

m. $$\lim_{x\to 1}\left(\sqrt{x^2-1}\right)=\sqrt{(1)^2-1}=0$$

CHAPTER 9 - THE METHOD OF APPROXIMATION AND DEFINING INSTANTANEOUS SPEED

ANSWERS TO THE STUDY QUESTIONS

1. What are the three central concepts of calculus? What is the law that ties them all together? Why is the limit perhaps the most important of all three?

   The three central concepts of calculus are the limit of the function, the derivative of a function, and the integral of a function. The law that ties them all together is the Fundamental Theorem of Calculus. The limit is perhaps the most important of all three because the other two are defined in terms of limits.

2. Why are we so interested in calculus?

   We are so interested in calculus because we're interested in one of the central problems in philosophy and science: the problem of change. We are interested in calculus because it will help us to understand Western intellectual history.

3. What is the main goal of this chapter?

   The main goal of this chapter is to apply our new tool of limits to the concept of speed to arrive at a coherent definition of instantaneous speed.

4. Explain the paradox of speed.

   The paradox of speed is that an object in motion is clearly in motion at any given instant. Yet in an instant, no time elapses, and what's more, if no time elapses, then the object doesn't have any time to move. To determine an objects speed, we divide distance by time, but if we are looking at one instant, that would mean we need to divide 0 by 0, which is meaningless. But again, our experience tells us that the object is moving at every instant, so we are left with a paradox.

5. What is the ancient problem of change? (Think about the question Thales was trying to answer.)

The ancient problem of change, the question that Thales was trying to answer, is to explain why there is both change and order in the world.

6. Why is it easy to determine the instantaneous speed of an object when its speed is constant? Why doesn't this solve our paradox of speed?

   It is easy to determine the instantaneous speed of an object when its speed is constant because constant means that the objects speed does not change. So the object's speed at any given time interval will be the same as its speed at any given instant. This doesn't solve our paradox of speed because we still don't know what instantaneous speed *is* or how to calculate for *any* case.

7. Write the definition of average speed in delta notation.

$$v_{ave} = \frac{\Delta d}{\Delta t}$$

8. Write the definition of average speed in terms of initial and final times and distances.

$$v_{ave} = \frac{d_f - d_i}{t_f - t_i}$$

9. In the example, why did I write the distances as d_1 and d_3 rather than d_i and d_f?

   In the example, you wrote the distances as d_1 and d_3 rather than d_i and d_f to remind us that d_1 is the distance that the ball travels in 1 second, and d_3 is the distance that the ball travels in 3 seconds.

10. What is acceleration?

    Acceleration means that a speed is not constant, or that the speed is changing.

11. For a dropped object the average velocity between 1 and 3 seconds is smaller than the average velocity between the interval covering 2 to 3 seconds. Why is the latter average speed greater even though the interval is smaller?

    If we calculate the average velocity for a dropped object between 0 and 3 seconds, and we also calculate the average velocity for the same dropped object between 2 and 3 seconds, we find that the average velocity of the second situation is larger than the average velocity of the first, even though the time

interval is smaller (3 seconds in the first case and 1 second in the latter). This is because in the second case we are looking at a period of the fall nearer to the end, when the object is moving faster, which makes the average velocity larger. When we look at the interval of time from 0 to 3 seconds, we are including the velocity of the object when it was first dropped, which is 0. This will bring the average velocity down. When we look at the interval of time from 2 to 3 seconds, we are not including that point in time when the object was stationary, in fact, the object is already moving fast at 2 seconds, so the average velocity is larger.

12. In words, describe the method of approximation for finding (i.e., approximating) instantaneous speed at some particular instant.

    Using the method of approximation, we can find the instantaneous speed at some particular instant by calculating the average speed over smaller and smaller time intervals near the particular instant. As the time interval approaches 0 seconds, the average velocity approaches the instantaneous velocity at the particular instant.

13. In the method of approximation, how small can you make the time interval, Δt?

    In the method of approximation, we can make the time interval Δt as small as we want, depending on how accurate we wish to be.

14. In the method of approximation, why do we calculate the average speed for multiple time intervals rather than for a single time interval?

    In the method of approximation, we calculate the average speed for multiple time intervals rather than for a single time interval so that we can see the path (metaphorically speaking) that the average speed is taking as it approaches instantaneous speed.

15. In symbols, represent the phrase, "The limit of the average velocity as delta t approaches zero is ninety-six feet per second."

$$\lim_{\Delta t \to 0} v_{ave} = 96\, ft / s$$

16. Complete the following sentence: "As Δt approaches 0, the average velocity approaches the ________________________."

"As Δt approaches 0, the average velocity approaches the <u>instantaneous velocity.</u>"

17. Define instantaneous speed/velocity in words (remember we're using 'speed' and 'velocity' as synonyms in this book).

Instantaneous velocity is the limit of the average velocity as Δt approaches 0.

18. Define instantaneous speed/velocity in symbols.

$$v = \lim_{\Delta t \to 0} (v_{ave}) = \lim_{\Delta t \to 0} \left(\frac{\Delta d}{\Delta t} \right)$$

EXERCISE SOLUTIONS

1) $$v_{ave} = \frac{\Delta d}{\Delta t} = \frac{d(1)-d(.5)}{1-.5} = \frac{16(1)^2-16(.5)^2}{.5} = \frac{16-4}{0.5} = \frac{12}{5} = 24 \text{ ft/s}$$

2) $$v_{ave} = \frac{\Delta d}{\Delta t} = \frac{d(1)-d(.5)}{1-.5} = 24 \text{ ft/s} \quad \text{From (1)}$$

$$v_{ave} = \frac{d(1)-d(.75)}{1-.75} = \frac{16(1)^2-16(.75)^2}{.25} = \frac{16-9}{.25} = 28 \text{ ft/s}$$

$$v_{ave} = \frac{d(1)-d(.9)}{1-.9} = \frac{16(1)^2-16(.9)^2}{.1} = \frac{16-12.96}{1} = 30.4 \text{ ft/s}$$

$$v_{ave} = \frac{d(1)-d(.99)}{1-.99} = \frac{16(1)^2-16(.99)^2}{.01} = \frac{16-15.68}{.01} = 31.84 \text{ ft/s}$$

$$v_{ave} = \frac{d(1)-d(.999)}{1-.999} = \frac{16(1)^2-16(.999)^2}{.001} = \frac{16-15.968}{.001} = 31.98 \text{ ft/s}$$

$$v_{ave} = \frac{d(1)-d(.9999)}{1-.9999} = \frac{16(1)^2-16(.9999)^2}{.0001} = \frac{16-15.997}{.0001} = 32.00 \text{ ft/s}$$

Approaching 32 ft/s.

$d = 16(1)^2 = 16$ ft

3) $v_{ave} = \frac{\Delta d}{\Delta t} = \frac{d(2)-d(1.75)}{2-1.75} = \frac{16(2)^2-16(1.75)^2}{.25} = \frac{64-49}{.25} = 60 \text{ ft/s}$

$$v_{ave} = \frac{d(2)-d(1.9)}{2-1.9} = \frac{16(2)^2-16(1.9)^2}{.1} = \frac{64-57.6}{.1} = 62.4 \text{ ft/s}$$

$$v_{ave} = \frac{d(2)-d(1.99)}{2-1.99} = \frac{16(2)^2-16(1.99)^2}{.01} = \frac{64-63.36}{.01} = 63.84 \text{ ft/s}$$

$$v_{ave} = \frac{d(2)-d(1.999)}{2-1.999} = \frac{16(2)^2-16(1.999)^2}{.001} = \frac{64-63.936}{.001} = 63.984 \text{ ft/s}$$

$$v_{ave} = \frac{d(2)-d(1.9999)}{2-1.9999} = \frac{16(2)^2-16(1.9999)^2}{.0001} = \frac{64-63.994}{.0001} = 64.00 \text{ ft/s}$$

Approaching 64 ft/s.

$d = 16(2)^2 = 64 \text{ ft}$

4) $v_{ave} = \frac{d(8)-d(7.75)}{8-7.75} = \frac{16(8)^2-16(7.75)^2}{.25} = \frac{1024-961}{.25} = 252 \text{ ft/s}$

$$v_{ave} = \frac{16(8)^2-16(7.9)^2}{8-7.9} = \frac{1024-998.56}{.1} = 254.4 \text{ ft/s}$$

$$v_{ave} = \frac{16(8)^2-16(7.99)^2}{8-7.99} = \frac{1024-1021.442}{.01} = 255.84 \text{ ft/s}$$

$$v_{ave} = \frac{16(8)^2-16(7.999)^2}{8-7.999} = \frac{1024-1023.744}{.001} = 255.984 \text{ ft/s}$$

$$v_{ave} = \frac{16(8)^2-16(7.999)^2}{8-7.999} = \frac{1024-1023.974}{.0001} = 256.00 \text{ ft/s}$$

Approaching 256 ft/s.

$d = 16(8)^2 = 1024 \text{ ft}$

CHAPTER 10 - USING THE METHOD OF INCREMENTS TO CALCULATE INSTANTANEOUS SPEED

ANSWERS TO THE STUDY QUESTIONS

1. What is the ancient and ongoing problem that calculus helps humans address?

   The ancient and ongoing problem that calculus helps humans address is the problem of change.

2. What is the Platonic-Pythagorean project?

   The Platonic-Pythagorean project is to describe the universe mathematically.

3. Write the definition of instantaneous speed in symbols. What does this mean in words?

   In symbols the definition of instantaneous speed is, $v = \lim_{\Delta t \to 0} (v_{ave}) = \lim_{\Delta t \to 0} \left(\frac{\Delta d}{\Delta t} \right)$. In words this means, Instantaneous velocity is the limit of the average velocity as Δt approaches 0, or, instantaneous velocity is the limit of the change in distance over the change in time as Δt approaches 0.

4. Why are we going to use v rather than v_{inst} to represent instantaneous speed?

   We are going to use v to represent instantaneous speed instead of v_{ins} since it's simpler and we already have a way to distinguish v from average velocity—that is, by using v_{ave}.

5. What does $d(t_i)$ mean?

   $d(t_i)$ means that distance is a function of the initial time, or we could say the distance evaluated at the initial time.

6. In our first example, what do t_i and t_f mean? What do d_i and d_f mean?

   In our first example, t_i means the initial time, and means the final time, in this case, 3 seconds. means the initial distance, and means the final distance, in this case, 144 feet.

7. In our first example, where did we get $t_i = 3-\Delta t$? How did we get $d_i = 16(3-\Delta t)^2$? How did we find $d_f = 144$ ft? Where did we get $t_f = 3$ seconds?

   a. **In our first example, we said that $t_i = 3-\Delta t$. We got this by rearranging the formula $\Delta t = t_f - t_i$ and remembering that in this case, $t_f = 3$.**

   b. **We said that $d_i = 16(3-\Delta t)^2$. We got this by plugging in our new formula for t_i($t_i = 3-\Delta t$) into the free fall formula ($d = 16t^2$).**

   c. **We found $d_f = 144\,ft$ by plugging 3 seconds into our free fall formula.**

   d. **We said that $t_f = 3$ seconds because 3 seconds is our instant of interest.**

8. Why did we need to keep Δt in our formula for average velocity?

   We needed to keep Δt in our formula for average velocity because our definition for instantaneous speed is $v = \lim_{\Delta t \to 0} (v_{ave})$ and the limit we're interested in is "as Δt approaches 0."

9. What are we calling the procedure we used in this chapter to find the instantaneous speed? Where did most of the work come in?

   We are calling the procedure we used in this chapter to find the instantaneous speed the Method of Increments. Most of the work in this procedure came from finding a formula for $\Delta d/\Delta t$ and most of the work in finding the formula was figuring out what form of the instants, t_f and t_i, to plug in for d.

10. What are the two steps of the Method of Increments?

    The two steps of the Method of Increments are first, find a formula for $\Delta d/\Delta t$, and second, take the limit of $\Delta d/\Delta t$ as Δt approaches 0.

11. In a single sentence, what is the general procedure for finding instantaneous speed?

    The general procedure for finding instantaneous speed is to find a formula for $\Delta d/\Delta t$ where Δt is no longer in the denominator, then substitute 0 for Δt.

12. In our second example, where we approached the instant of interest from the opposite direction, what was t_i and how is this different from the t_i in the previous example? What were d_f and t_f? How did we find $d_i = 144$ ft? Where did we get $t_i = 3$ seconds?

a. **In our second example, t_i was 3 seconds. This is different from our previous example where t_i was equal to $t_f - \Delta t$.**

b. **t_f was = $3+\Delta t$ +and d_f was $16(3+\Delta t)^2$.**

c. **We found d_i =144 *ft* by plugging 3 seconds into our free fall formula.**

d. **We said that t_i = 3 seconds because 3 seconds is our instant of interest.**

13. In the chapter we used the Method of Increments to calculate a number. What will we use this method to calculate in the next chapter?

In the next chapter, we will use the Method of Increments to find a function that will allow us to calculate instantaneous speed at many different instants.

EXERCISE SOLUTIONS

1) See exercise (4) from Chapter 9.

2)
$$\frac{\Delta d}{\Delta t} = \frac{d(8)-d(8-\Delta t)}{\Delta t} = \frac{16(8)^2-16(8-\Delta t)^2}{\Delta t} = \frac{1024-16(8-\Delta t)(8-\Delta t)}{\Delta t} =$$
$$= \frac{1024-16(64-8\Delta t-8\Delta t+(\Delta t)^2)}{\Delta t} = \frac{1024-16(64-16\Delta t+(\Delta t)^2)}{\Delta t} =$$
$$= \frac{1024-1024+256\Delta t-16(\Delta t)^2}{\Delta t} = \frac{256\Delta t-16(\Delta t)^2}{\Delta t} =$$
$$= 256-16\Delta t \qquad (\Delta t \neq 0)$$
$$v_8 = \lim_{\Delta t \to 0}(v_{ave}) = \lim_{\Delta t \to 0}(256-16\Delta t) = 256 \text{ ft/s}$$

3)
$$\frac{\Delta d}{\Delta t} = \frac{d(1)-d(1-\Delta t)}{\Delta t} = \frac{16(1)^2-16(1-\Delta t)^2}{\Delta t} = \frac{16-16(1-\Delta t)(1-\Delta t)}{\Delta t} =$$
$$= \frac{16-16(1-2\Delta t+(\Delta t)^2)}{\Delta t} = \frac{16-16+32\Delta t-16(\Delta t)^2}{\Delta t} =$$
$$= \frac{32\Delta t-16(\Delta t)^2}{\Delta t} = 32-16\Delta t \qquad (\Delta t \neq 0)$$
$$v_1 = \lim_{\Delta t \to 0}(32-16\Delta t) = 32 \text{ ft/s}$$

4)
$$\frac{\Delta d}{\Delta t} = \frac{d(1+\Delta t)-d(1)}{\Delta t} = \frac{16(1+\Delta t)^2-16(1)^2}{\Delta t} = \frac{16(1+2\Delta t+(\Delta t)^2)-16}{\Delta t} =$$
$$= \frac{16+32\Delta t+16(\Delta t)^2-16}{\Delta t} = \frac{32\Delta t+16(\Delta t)^2}{\Delta t} = 32+16\Delta t \qquad (\Delta t \neq 0)$$
$$v_1 = \lim_{\Delta t \to 0}(32+16\Delta t) = 32 \text{ ft/s}$$

5) $$\frac{\Delta d}{\Delta t} = \frac{d(2) - d(2-\Delta t)}{\Delta t} = \frac{16(2)^2 - 16(2-\Delta t)^2}{\Delta t} = \frac{64 - 16(2-\Delta t)(2-\Delta t)}{\Delta t} =$$
$$= \frac{64 - 16(4 - 4\Delta t + (\Delta t)^2)}{\Delta t} = \frac{64 - 64 + 64\Delta t - 16(\Delta t)^2}{\Delta t} = \frac{64\Delta t - 16(\Delta t)^2}{\Delta t}$$
$$= 64 - 16\Delta t \qquad (\Delta t \neq 0)$$
$$v_2 = \lim_{\Delta t \to 0}(64 - 16\Delta t) = 64 \text{ ft/s}$$

6) $$\frac{\Delta d}{\Delta t} = \frac{d(2+\Delta t) - d(2)}{\Delta t} = \frac{16(2+\Delta t)^2 - 16(2)^2}{\Delta t} = \frac{16(2+\Delta t)(2+\Delta t) - 64}{\Delta t} =$$
$$= \frac{16(4 + 4\Delta t + (\Delta t)^2) - 64}{\Delta t} = \frac{64 + 64\Delta t + 16(\Delta t)^2 - 64}{\Delta t} = \frac{64\Delta t + 16(\Delta t)^2}{\Delta t} =$$
$$= 64 + 16\Delta t \qquad (\Delta t \neq 0)$$
$$v_2 = \lim_{\Delta t \to 0}(64 + 16\Delta t) = 64 \text{ ft/s}$$

CHAPTER 11 - USING THE METHOD OF INCREMENTS TO FIND AN INSTANTANEOUS SPEED FUNCTION

ANSWERS TO THE STUDY QUESTIONS

1. What is our goal in this chapter?

   Our goal in this chapter is to find an instantaneous speed function that is good for any value of t.

2. Does Galileo's law of fall work for a falling cat? For an anvil? For <your name here>?

   Galileo's law of fall works for a falling cat, a falling anvil, and for me (as long as air resistance isn't a factor).

3. What are the steps in the Method of Increments?

   The two steps of the Method of Increments are first, find a formula for $\Delta d/\Delta t$, and second, take the limit of $\Delta d/\Delta t$ as Δt approaches 0.

4. What physical quantity does $\Delta d/\Delta t$ represent? How do we define instantaneous speed in terms of this?

   $\Delta d/\Delta t$ represents average velocity. We define instantaneous speed as the limit of the average velocity as Δt approaches 0.

5. What method did we use to get the function $v(t)$?

   To get the function $v(t)$ we used the Method of Increments.

6. We now have two functions relating to falling objects near the earth's surface. What are they?

   We now have two functions relating to falling objects near the earth's surface. They are $d(t) = 16t^2$ and $v(t) = 32t$. The first function tells us how far an object has fallen in a given amount of time and the second function tells us an object's instantaneous speed at a given time.

7. Why ought we be amazed at our ability to arrive at a method for calculating instantaneous speed? How is this related to the Platonic-Pythagorean view of the world?

   We ought to be amazed at our ability to arrive at a method for calculating instantaneous speed because we arrived at a relation between instantaneous speed and time *without doing any experiments whatsoever.* This is an affirmation of the Platonic-Pythagorean view of the world that the world can be described mathematically because we discovered something true about the world using just mathematics.

8. Explain why someone might say that the universe is "user-friendly."

   We are able to manipulate symbols and numbers to arrive at knowledge of the physical world which is an amazing coincidence that might lead someone to say that the universe is "user-friendly."

9. Describe in words what the function $v(t)$ is and some of its benefits.

   $v(t)$ is the velocity function for any object that falls close to the earth's surface. It allows us to calculate an object's instantaneous speed at any given instant and it is laughably easy to use.

10. What are the three central concepts of calculus? What mathematical law ties them all together? Which have we studied so far? Which will we study in the next chapter?

    The three central concepts of calculus are: the limit of a function, the derivative of a function, and the integral of a function. The Fundamental Theorem of Calculus ties them all together. So far we have studied the limit of a function, and in the next chapter we will study the derivative of a function.

EXERCISE SOLUTIONS

1) $$\frac{\Delta d}{\Delta t}=\frac{d(t)-d(t-\Delta t)}{\Delta t}=\frac{16(t)^2-16(t-\Delta t)^2}{\Delta t}=\frac{16t^2-16(t-\Delta t)(t-\Delta t)}{\Delta t}=$$
$$=\frac{16t^2-16(t^2-2t\Delta t+(\Delta t)^2)}{\Delta t}=\frac{16t^2-16t^2+32t\Delta t-16(\Delta t)^2}{\Delta t}=$$
$$=\frac{32t\Delta t-16(\Delta t)^2}{\Delta t}=32t-16\Delta t$$
$$v(t)=\lim_{\Delta t\to 0}v_{ave}=\lim_{\Delta t\to 0}\frac{\Delta d}{\Delta t}=\lim_{\Delta t\to 0}(32t-16\Delta t)=32t$$

2) a. $v(1)=32(1)=32$ ft/s; $d(1)=16(1)^2=16$ ft
b. $v(2)=32(2)=64$ ft/s; $d(2)=16(2)^2=64$ ft
c. $v(7)=32(7)=224$ ft/s; $d(7)=16(7)^2=784$ ft

3) $$\frac{\Delta d}{\Delta t}=\frac{d(t+\Delta t)-d(t)}{\Delta t}=\frac{6(t+\Delta t)^2-6(t)^2}{\Delta t}=\frac{6(t+\Delta t)(t+\Delta t)-6t^2}{\Delta t}$$
$$=\frac{6(t^2+2t\Delta t+(\Delta t)^2)-6t^2}{\Delta t}=\frac{6t^2+12t\Delta t+6(\Delta t)^2-6t^2}{\Delta t}$$
$$=\frac{12t\Delta t+6(\Delta t)^2}{\Delta t}=12t+6\Delta t$$
$$v(t)=\lim_{\Delta t\to 0}(12t+6\Delta t)=12t$$

4) a. $v(1)=12(1)=12$ ft/s; $d(1)=6(1)^2=6$ ft
b. $v(2)=12(2)=24$ ft/s; $d(2)=6(2)^2=24$ ft
c. $v(7)=12(7)=84$ ft/s; $d(7)=6(7)^2=294$ ft

5) $$\frac{\Delta d}{\Delta t}=\frac{d(t)-d(t-\Delta t)}{\Delta t}=\frac{40(t)^2-40(t-\Delta t)^2}{\Delta t}=\frac{40t^2-40(t-\Delta t)(t-\Delta t)}{\Delta t}$$
$$=\frac{40t^2-40(t^2-2t\Delta t+(\Delta t)^2)}{\Delta t}=\frac{40t^2-40t^2+80t\Delta t-40(\Delta t)^2}{\Delta t}$$
$$=\frac{80t\Delta t-40(\Delta t)^2}{\Delta t}=80t-40\Delta t$$
$$v(t)=\lim_{\Delta t\to 0}(80t-40\Delta t)=80t$$

6) a. $v(1)=80(1)=80$ ft/s; $d(1)=40(1)^2=40$ ft
b. $v(2)=80(2)=160$ ft/s; $d(2)=40(2)^2=160$ ft
c. $v(7)=80(7)=560$ ft/s; $d(7)=40(7)^2=1960$ ft

7) $$\frac{\Delta d}{\Delta t} = \frac{d(t+\Delta t)-d(t)}{\Delta t} = \frac{\frac{g}{2}(t-\Delta t)^2 - \frac{g}{2}(t)^2}{\Delta t} = \frac{\frac{g}{2}(t+\Delta t)(t+\Delta t) - \frac{g}{2}t^2}{\Delta t}$$

$$= \frac{\frac{g}{2}(t^2 + 2t\Delta t + (\Delta t)^2) - \frac{g}{2}t^2}{\Delta t} = \frac{\frac{g}{2}t^2 + \frac{g}{2}\cdot 2t\Delta t + \frac{g}{2}(\Delta t)^2 - \frac{g}{2}t^2}{\Delta t}$$

$$= \frac{gt\Delta t + \frac{g}{2}(\Delta t)^2}{\Delta t} = gt + \frac{g}{2}\Delta t$$

$$v(t) = \lim_{\Delta t \to 0} (gt + \frac{g}{2}\Delta t) = gt$$

CHAPTER 12 - THE DERIVATIVE

ANSWERS TO THE STUDY QUESTIONS

1. In symbols, what is the definition of instantaneous speed, $v(t)$? What is the process for calculating it?

   In symbols, the definition of instantaneous speed is $v = \lim_{\Delta t \to 0} (v_{ave}) = \lim_{\Delta t \to 0} \left(\frac{\Delta d}{\Delta t} \right)$. The process for calculating instantaneous speed is called the Method of Increments.

2. What are the three central concepts of calculus? What theorem ties them all together?

   The three central concepts of calculus are the limit, the derivative, and the integral. The Fundamental Theorem of Calculus ties them all together.

3. Why do we use the word "derivative"? What other related terms will we use to talk about the process of finding derivatives?

   We use the word "derivative" because in finding the derivative of a function we derive one function from another. We can also say that we *differentiate* a function to find its derivative. Another related phrase we will use to talk about the derivative is "with respect to."

4. What is the definition of instantaneous speed in terms of the derivative of a function?

   The definition of instantaneous speed in terms of the derivative of a function is, v = the derivative of $d(t) = \lim_{\Delta t \to 0} \left(\frac{\Delta d}{\Delta t} \right)$.

5. In terms of "input" and "output," what is the difference between independent and dependent variables? In what sense is the dependent variable dependent?

   The independent variable is the input of the function, and the dependent variable is the output. The dependent variable is dependent because its value *depends* upon the input.

6. In $d(t)$ what is the independent variable?

   In $d(t)$ the independent variable is t. That is, the distance that a falling object travels depends on the time the object has been falling for.

7. In terms of dependent and independent variables what is the definition of a derivative? (This was the complicated version.) Now write it in symbols, using $y(x)$.

   In terms of dependent and independent variables, the definition of a derivative is "the limit of the rate of change in the dependent variable with respect to the independent variable as the change in the independent variable approaches 0." In symbols, using $y(x)$, this is, the derivative of $y(x) = \lim_{\Delta x \to 0} \left(\frac{\Delta y}{\Delta x} \right)$.

8. What are the two main steps for finding the derivative of a function $y(x)$?

   The two main steps for finding the derivative of a function $y(x)$ are to find a formula for $\frac{\Delta y}{\Delta x}$ and then to take the limit of $\frac{\Delta y}{\Delta x}$ as Δx approaches 0.

9. In terms of "rate of change" what is instantaneous speed?

   In terms of "rate of change," instantaneous speed is the instantaneous rate of change in location with respect to time.

10. In terms of "rate of change" what is calculus?

    In terms of "rate of change," calculus is the mathematics of instantaneous rates of change.

11. Is the rate in "rate of change" always about a change in time? Explain.

    The rate in "rate of change" is not always about a change in time. For example, the air temperature might change the higher in the atmosphere you go. In this case, we would speak of the rate of change in temperature with respect to altitude.

12. In terms of "independent variable" what does an "instant" mean generally (and not just for time)?

    In terms of "independent variable," "instant" generally means when the interval of the independent variable approaches 0, or, when the independent variable's interval becomes *infinitesimally small*.

13. Express, "The instantaneous rate of change in y with respect to x" using symbols.

$$\lim_{\Delta x \to 0}\left(\frac{\Delta y}{\Delta x}\right)$$

14. Express, "The average rate of change in y with respect to x" using symbols.

$$\frac{\Delta y}{\Delta x}$$

15. Write out the steps of the Method of Increments using the phrase, "rate of change."

    First, find a formula for the average rate of change, $\frac{\Delta y}{\Delta x}$, and second, take the limit of $\frac{\Delta y}{\Delta x}$ as Δx approaches 0 to find the instantaneous rate of change.

16. Explain the following:

$$\lim_{\Delta x \to 0}\left(\frac{\Delta y}{\Delta x}\right) \neq \lim_{x \to 0} y(x)$$

    There are two main reasons why these are not the same. The first is that the limit is being performed on two different functions, namely $\frac{\Delta y}{\Delta x}$ and $y(x)$. The second is that the independent variables that approach 0 are different, namely Δx and x.

17. Are all derivatives limits? Are all limits derivatives?

    All derivatives are limits, but not all limits are derivatives.

18. What are some ways to express (in symbols) the derivative of $y(x)$?

    Some ways to express the derivative of $y(x)$ in symbols are y', $\frac{dy}{dx}$, and $\lim_{\Delta x \to 0} \frac{\Delta y}{\Delta x}$.

19. What will we do in the next chapter?

    In the next chapter, we will use the Method of Increments to find the derivative of any function that has the form $y(x) = ax^2 + bx + c$. We'll also look at the idea of taking the derivative of derivatives.

EXERCISE SOLUTIONS

1) $y(x) = 5x^2$

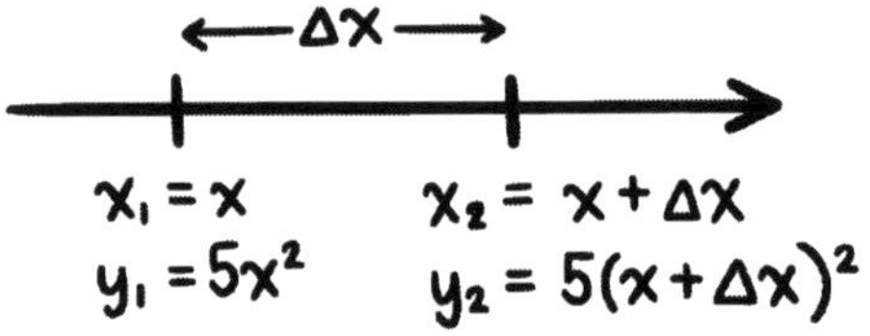

$\leftarrow \Delta x \rightarrow$

$x_1 = x$ $\quad$ $x_2 = x + \Delta x$

$y_1 = 5x^2$ $\quad$ $y_2 = 5(x+\Delta x)^2$

$$\frac{\Delta y}{\Delta x} = \frac{y(x+\Delta x) - y(x)}{\Delta x} = \frac{5(x+\Delta x)^2 - 5(x)^2}{\Delta x} = \frac{5(x+\Delta x)(x+\Delta x) - 5x^2}{\Delta x}$$
$$= \frac{5(x^2 + 2x\Delta x + (\Delta x)^2) - 5x^2}{\Delta x} = \frac{5x^2 + 10x\Delta x + 5(\Delta x)^2 - 5x^2}{\Delta x}$$
$$= \frac{10x\Delta x + 5(\Delta x)^2}{\Delta x} = 10x + 5\Delta x$$

$$y'(x) = \frac{dy}{dx} = \lim_{\Delta x \to 0}\left(\frac{\Delta y}{\Delta x}\right) = \lim_{\Delta x \to 0}(10x + 5\Delta x) = 10x$$

2) $y(x) = 5x^2 \quad \Rightarrow \quad \left.\frac{dy}{dx}\right|_{x=3} = y'(3) = 10(3) = 30$

3) $y = 3x$

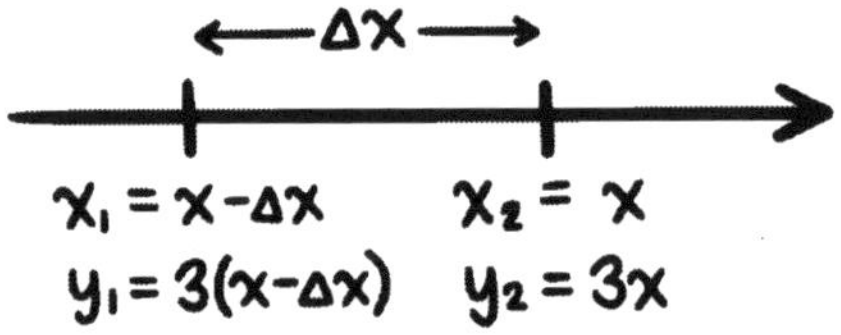

$\leftarrow \Delta x \rightarrow$

$x_1 = x - \Delta x$ $\quad$ $x_2 = x$

$y_1 = 3(x - \Delta x)$ $\quad$ $y_2 = 3x$

$$\frac{\Delta y}{\Delta x} = \frac{y(x) - y(x-\Delta x)}{\Delta x} = \frac{3x - 3(x-\Delta x)}{\Delta x} = \frac{3x - 3x + 3\Delta x}{\Delta x} =$$
$$= \frac{3\Delta x}{\Delta x} = 3$$
$$y' = \lim_{\Delta x \to 0} 3 = 3 \qquad y' = 3$$

4) $\lim_{x \to 3} y(x) = \lim_{x \to 3} 5x^2 = 5(3)^2 = 5 \cdot 9 = 45$

5) $f(x) = 2x^3$

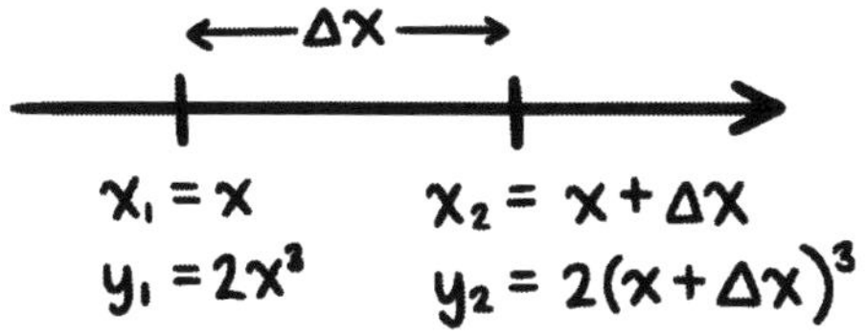

Δx

$x_1 = x$ $\quad$ $x_2 = x + \Delta x$

$y_1 = 2x^3$ $\quad$ $y_2 = 2(x + \Delta x)^3$

$$\frac{\Delta y}{\Delta x} = \frac{y(x+\Delta x) - y(x)}{\Delta x} = \frac{2(x+\Delta x)^3 - 2(x)^3}{\Delta x} = \frac{2(x+\Delta x)(x+\Delta x)(x+\Delta x) - 2x^3}{\Delta x}$$

$$= \frac{2(x^3 + 2x\Delta x + x(\Delta x)^2(x+\Delta x) - 2x^3}{\Delta x} =$$

$$= \frac{2(x^3 + 2x^2\Delta x + x(\Delta x)^2 + x^2\Delta x + 2x(\Delta x)^2 + (\Delta x)^3) - 2x^3}{\Delta x} =$$

$$= \frac{\cancel{2x^3} + \cancel{4x^2\Delta x}\ \cancel{2x(\Delta x)^2} + \cancel{2x^2\Delta x} + \cancel{4x(\Delta x)^2} + 2(\Delta x)^3 - \cancel{2x^3}}{\Delta x} =$$

$$= \frac{6x^2\Delta x + 6x(\Delta x)^2 + 2(\Delta x)^3}{\Delta x} = 6x^2 + 6x\Delta x + 2(\Delta x)^2$$

$f'(x)$ is the function that gives the instantaneous rate of change for $f(x) = 2x^3$, and so $f'(x) = \lim_{\Delta x \to 0} (6x^2 + 6x\Delta x + 2(\Delta x)^2) = 6x^2$.

CHAPTER 13 - FINDING MORE DERIVATIVES

ANSWERS TO THE STUDY QUESTIONS

1. What is the definition of a derivative?

   The definition of a derivative is $y'(x) = \lim_{\Delta x \to 0} \frac{\Delta y}{\Delta x}$.

2. What is the general form of functions that we're considering in this chapter? Give some specific examples of functions in this form.

   The general form of functions that we're considering in this chapter is $y(x) = ax^2 + bx + c$. Some examples of functions in this form are, $y(x) = 7x^2 + 3x + 1$, $y(x) = 6$, and $y(x) = 6$.

3. What are some of the names for functions like $y(x) = ax^2 + bx + c$? Explain each of the names.

   Some of the names for functions like $y(x) = ax^2 + bx + c$ are *polynomials*, *quadratic functions*, and *second-order polynomials*. *Polynomials* means "many names" or "many terms", *quadratic* comes from the Latin for "square," and we use that term because of the x^2, or in words, "x squared," and *second-order* refers to the fact that the highest degree of the polynomial is 2, that is, the highest exponent is 2.

4. For our purposes of learning the derivative for functions with the form $y(x) = ax^2 + bx + c$, what is the restriction we're putting on *a, b, and c* and why are we putting that restriction on them?

   The restriction that we put on *a* is that it is a constant, it can be any number whatsoever, except for 0, since that would leave us without anything to differentiate.

5. What is the derivative of any function of the form $y(x) = ax^2$ (in the exercises you'll be asked to derive this using the Method of Increments)?

   The derivative of any function of the form $y(x) = ax^2$ is $y'(x) = 2ax$.

6. How was using the Method of Increments on $y(x) = ax^2$ kind of like calculating an infinite number of derivatives?

   Using the Method of increments on $y(x) = ax^2$ was kind of like calculating an infinite number of derivatives because by performing the derivation on the general form of the function, we effectively did an infinite number of derivations, one for each specific function of the form, and one for each value of x.

7. Why is bx called a "first-order" term?

   bx is called a first-order term because its highest degree is 1, that is, the highest exponent is 1. We could rewrite bx as bx^1 .

8. If a function has a constant derivative, does that mean that the function's value—its dependent value—doesn't change? Explain.

   If a function has a constant derivative, that does not mean that the function's value—its dependent value—isn't changing. Instead, it means that the function's value is changing uniformly. For example, if we were to look at a car traveling at a constant rate of 50 miles per hour, the function $d(t)=50t$ would give us the distance traveled. The dependent value, the distance, would change over time, but the derivative, in this case the car's instantaneous speed, would always be 50 miles per hour.

9. How might you write $y(x) = c$ as a function of x?

   $y(x) = c$ can be written as a function of x in this way: $y(x)= cx^0$. We remember that anything to the power of 0 is 1 and since anything multiplied by 1 is itself, we have two functions stated differently that mean the same thing—one with the x and one without.

10. For the function $y(x) = c$ and its derivative, $y'(x) = 0$, the values for $y(x)$ and $y'(x)$ are both constant. And yet they're different. In what way?

    For the functions $y(x) = c$ and $y'(x) = 0$, the values for $y(x)$ and $y'(x)$ are both constants. Even though both values are constants, they tell us different things. In the example of a cyclist, we had the velocity function . This tells us that the cyclist is traveling at 15 miles per hour. The derivative of this function

would be $v'(t)=0$. This tells us how fast the cyclist's speed is changing—that is, not at all.

11. In terms of our prime notation, how would you denote the derivative of $y(x) = f(x) + g(x) + u(x)$?

    In terms of our prime notation, the derivative of $y(x) = f(x) + g(x) + u(x)$ would be $y'(x) = f'(x) + g'(x) + u'(x)$.

12. What is the first, second, and third derivative of $y(x) = ax^2 + bx + c$?

    The first derivative of $y(x) = ax^2 + bx + c$ is $y'(x) = 2ax + b$. The second derivative is $y''(x) = 2a$, and the third derivative is $y'''(x) = 0$.

13. What will we do in the next chapter?

    In the next chapter, we will learn how to take the derivative of any function with the form $y(x) = an^2$, where n is any constant.

EXERCISE SOLUTIONS

1) $y(x) = ax^2$

$$\frac{\Delta y}{\Delta x} = \frac{y(x) - y(x - \Delta x)}{\Delta x} = \frac{ax^2 - a(x - \Delta x)^2}{\Delta x} = \frac{ax^2 - a(x - \Delta x)(x - \Delta x)}{\Delta x} =$$

$$= \frac{ax^2 - a(x^2 - 2x\Delta x + (\Delta x)^2)}{\Delta x} = \frac{ax^2 - ax^2 + 2ax\Delta x - a(\Delta x)^2}{\Delta x} =$$

$$= \frac{2ax\Delta x - a(\Delta x)^2}{\Delta x} = 2ax - a\Delta x \qquad (\Delta x \neq 0)$$

$$\frac{dy}{dx} = \lim_{\Delta x \to 0}\left[\frac{\Delta y}{\Delta x}\right] = \lim_{\Delta x \to 0}(2ax - a\Delta x) = 2ax = \frac{dy}{dx}$$

2) $y(x) = ax^2$

$$\frac{\Delta y}{\Delta x} = \frac{y(x + \Delta x) - y(x)}{\Delta x} = \frac{a(x + \Delta x)^2 - ax^2}{\Delta x} =$$

$$= \frac{a(x + \Delta x)(x + \Delta x) - ax^2}{\Delta x} = \frac{a(x^2 + 2x\Delta x + (\Delta x)^2) - ax^2}{\Delta x} =$$

$$= \frac{ax^2 + 2ax\Delta x + a(\Delta x)^2 - ax^2}{\Delta x} = \frac{2ax\Delta x - a(\Delta x)^2}{\Delta x} = 2ax + a\Delta x$$

$(\Delta x \neq 0)$

$$\frac{dy}{dx} = \lim_{\Delta x \to 0}\left[\frac{\Delta y}{\Delta x}\right] = \lim_{\Delta x \to 0}\left(2ax + a\Delta x\right) = 2ax = \frac{dy}{dx}$$

3) a. $y(x) = 5x^2 \Rightarrow a = 5 \Rightarrow y'(x) = 2 \cdot 5x = 10x$

b. $f(x) = x^2 \Rightarrow a = 1 \Rightarrow f'(x) = 2 \cdot 1x = 2x$

c. $h(t) = -16t^2 \Rightarrow a = -16 \Rightarrow \dfrac{dh}{dt} = 2(-16)t = -32t$

d. $g(z) = \dfrac{15}{\pi} \Rightarrow a = \dfrac{15}{\pi} \Rightarrow g'(z) = 2\left[\dfrac{15}{\pi}\right]z = \dfrac{30}{\pi}z$

4) $y(x) = bx$

$$\frac{\Delta y}{\Delta x} = \frac{y(x) - y(x - \Delta x)}{\Delta x} = \frac{bx - b(x - \Delta x)}{\Delta x} = \frac{bx - bx + b\Delta x}{\Delta x} = \frac{b\Delta x}{\Delta x} = b$$

$(\Delta x \neq 0)$

$$\frac{dy}{dx} = \lim_{\Delta x \to 0}\left[\frac{\Delta y}{\Delta x}\right] = \lim_{\Delta x \to 0}(b) = b = \frac{dy}{dx}$$

(y changes, but at the constant rate of b.)

5) $y(x) = bx$

$$\frac{\Delta y}{\Delta x} = \frac{y(x + \Delta x) - y(x)}{\Delta x} = \frac{b(x + \Delta x) - bx}{\Delta x} = \frac{bx + b\Delta x - bx}{\Delta x} = \frac{b\Delta x}{\Delta x} = b$$

$(\Delta x \neq 0)$

$$\frac{dy}{dx} = \lim_{\Delta x \to 0}\left[\frac{\Delta y}{\Delta x}\right] = \lim_{\Delta x \to 0}(b) = b = \frac{dy}{dx}$$

6) a. $g(z) = 13x \Rightarrow b = 13 \Rightarrow g'(z) = 13$

b. $f(x) = x \Rightarrow b = 1 \Rightarrow f'(x) = 1$

c. $v(t) = -32t \Rightarrow b = -32 \Rightarrow v'(t) = -32$

d. $y(u) = \left(\sqrt[3]{2} - 1\right)u \Rightarrow b = \sqrt[3]{2} - 1 \Rightarrow y'(u) = \sqrt[3]{2} - 1$

7) $y(x) = c$

$$\frac{\Delta y}{\Delta x} = \frac{y(x) - y(x - \Delta x)}{\Delta x} = \frac{c - c}{\Delta x} = 0 \qquad (\Delta x \neq 0)$$

$$\frac{dy}{dx} = \lim_{\Delta x \to 0}\left[\frac{\Delta y}{\Delta x}\right] = \lim_{\Delta x \to 0} 0 = 0 = \frac{dy}{dx}$$

8) $y(x) = c$

$$\frac{\Delta y}{\Delta x} = \frac{y(x+\Delta x) - y(x)}{\Delta x} = \frac{c-c}{\Delta x} = 0 \qquad (\Delta x \neq 0)$$

$$\frac{dy}{dx} = \lim_{\Delta x \to 0}\left[\frac{\Delta y}{\Delta x}\right] = \lim_{\Delta x \to}(0) = 0 = \frac{dy}{dx}$$

9) a. $z(x) = 7 \Rightarrow c = 7 \Rightarrow z'(x) = 0$

b. $f(x) = 1 \Rightarrow c = 1 \Rightarrow f'(x) = 0$

c. $a(t) = -32 \Rightarrow c = -32 \Rightarrow a'(t) = 0$

d. $g(u) = \sqrt[3]{2} - 1 \Rightarrow c = \sqrt[3]{2} - 1 \Rightarrow g'(u) = 0$

10) $f(x) = 7x^2 + 3x + 1 \Rightarrow a = 7, \quad b = 3, \quad c = 1$

$$\frac{df}{dx} = 2(7)x + 3 = 14x + 3 \Rightarrow b = 14, \ c = 3$$

$$\frac{d^2 f}{dx^2} = 14 \Rightarrow c = 14$$

$$\frac{d^3 f}{dx^3} = 0$$

11) $g(x) = 3x^2 + 2x + 7 \Rightarrow a = 3, \ b = 2, \ c = 7$

$g'(x) = 3(2)x + 2 + 0 = 6x + 2 \Rightarrow b = 6; \quad c = 2$

$g''(x) = 6 \Rightarrow c = 6$

$g'''(x) = 0$

CHAPTER 14 - USING THE POWER RULE TO FIND DERIVATIVES

ANSWERS TO THE STUDY QUESTIONS

1. What was the previous chapter's main result?

   In the previous chapter we found an easier way to find the derivative of any function of the form $y(x) = ax^2 + bx + c$.

2. Write the general form of a power function.

   The general form of a power function is $f(x) = Kx^n$.

3. What is the difference between a polynomial and a power function?

   A polynomial can only have positive integers as exponents, whereas there is no such restriction on the exponents of power functions.

4. State the Power Rule.

   For any power function, $f(x) = Kx^n$, its derivative is $f'(x) = nKx^{n-1}$.

5. What is the rule for taking the derivative of the *sum* of power functions?

   For $y(x) = f(x) + g(x) + u(x)$... its derivative is $y'(x) = f'(x) + g'(x) + u'(x)$...

EXERCISE SOLUTIONS

1) a. $y(x) = 4x^3 \quad \Rightarrow \quad y' = 3 \cdot 4x^{3-1} = 12x^2$

   b. $d(t) = 16t^2 \quad \Rightarrow \quad d'(t) = 2 \cdot 16t^{2-1} = 32t$

   c. $v(t) = 32t \quad \Rightarrow \quad v'(t) = 1 \cdot 32t^{1-1} = 32$

   d. $a(t) = 32 = 32t^0 \quad \Rightarrow \quad a'(t) = 0 \cdot 32t^{0-1} = 0$

   e. $A(r) = \pi r^2 \quad \Rightarrow \quad A'(r) = 2 \cdot \pi r^{2-1} = 2\pi r$

   f. $V(r) = \frac{4}{3}\pi r^3 \quad \Rightarrow \quad \frac{dV}{dr} = 3\left[\frac{4}{3}\right]\pi r^{3-1} = 4\pi r^2$

   g. $d(t) = -16t^2 \Rightarrow d'(t) = 2(-16)t^{2-1} = -32t$

h. $y(x) = -16x^{-2} \quad \Rightarrow \quad y'(x) = -2\cdot(-16)x^{-2-1} = 32x^{-3} = \dfrac{32}{x^3}$

i. $y(x) = -16x^{-2} + 5x \quad \Rightarrow \quad y'(x) = -2\cdot(-16)x^{-2-1} + 1\cdot 5x^{1-1} =$

$=32x^{-3} + 5 = \dfrac{32}{x^3} + 5$

j. $g(x) = 5x^7 + 5x^5 \quad \Rightarrow \quad g'(x) = 7\cdot 5x^{7-1} + 5\cdot 5x^{5-1} = 35x^6 + 25x^4$

k. $f(x) = 4x^{10} \quad \Rightarrow \quad f'(x) = 10\cdot 4x^{10-1} = 40x^9$

l. $y(x) = 2x^{100} \quad \Rightarrow \quad \dfrac{dy}{dx} = 100\cdot 2x^{100-1} = 200x^{99}$

m. $z(x) = \dfrac{1}{x} = x^{-1} \quad \Rightarrow \quad z'(x) = -1\cdot x^{-1-1} = -x^{-2} = -\dfrac{1}{x^2}$

n. $y(x) = \dfrac{1}{x} + 4x^{16} + 9x^9 + 1 = -x^{-1} + 4x^{16} + 9x^9 + x^0$

$\Rightarrow \quad y'(x) = -1\cdot x^{-1-1} + 16\cdot 4x^{16-1} + 9\cdot 9x^{9-1} + 0\cdot x^{0-1} =$

$= -x^{-2} + 64x^{15} + 81x^8 = -\dfrac{1}{x^2} + 64x^{15} + 81x^8$

o. $y(x) = \dfrac{1}{x^4} + \dfrac{1}{x^3} + \dfrac{1}{x^2} + \dfrac{1}{x} = x^{-4} + x^{-3} + x^{-2} + x^{-1}$

$\Rightarrow \quad y'(x) = -4x^{-4-1} + (-3)x^{-3-1} + (-2)x^{-2-1} + (-1)x^{-1-1} =$

$= -4x^{-5} - 3x^{-4} - 2x^{-3} - x^{-2} = -\dfrac{4}{x^5} - \dfrac{3}{x^4} - \dfrac{2}{x^3} - \dfrac{1}{x^2}$

p. $g(x) = x^{-4} + x^{-3} + x^{-2} + x^{-1}$

$\Rightarrow \quad g'(x) = (-4)x^{-4-1} + (-3)x^{-3-1} + (-2)x^{-2-1} + (-1)x^{-1-1}$

$= -4x^{-5} - 3x^{-4} - 2x^{-3} - x^{-2} = -\dfrac{4}{x^5} - \dfrac{3}{x^4} - \dfrac{2}{x^3} - \dfrac{1}{x^2}$

q. $y(x) = \dfrac{8}{x^{-5}} + \dfrac{1}{x^{-1}} + \dfrac{55}{x^2} + \dfrac{4}{x} = 8x^5 + x + 55x^{-2} + 4x^{-1}$

$\Rightarrow \quad y'(x) = 5\cdot 8\cdot x^{5-1} + 1\cdot x^{1-1} + (-2)55x^{-2-1} + (-1)4x^{-1-1}$

$= 40x^4 + 1 - 110x^{-3} - 4x^{-2}$

$= 40x^4 + 1 - \dfrac{110}{x^3} - \dfrac{4}{x^2}$

r. $g(x) = \sqrt{x} = x^{\frac{1}{2}} \quad \Rightarrow \quad g'(x) = \dfrac{1}{2}x^{\frac{1}{2}-\frac{2}{2}} = \dfrac{1}{2}x^{-\frac{1}{2}} = \dfrac{1}{2x^{\frac{1}{2}}} = \dfrac{1}{2\sqrt{x}}$

s. $f(x) = 3\sqrt{x} = 3x^{\frac{1}{2}} \quad \Rightarrow \quad f'(x) = \dfrac{1}{2}(3)x^{\frac{1}{2}-\frac{2}{2}} = \dfrac{3}{2}x^{-\frac{1}{2}} = \dfrac{3}{2\sqrt{x}}$

t. $f(x) = \dfrac{17\sqrt{x}}{5} = \dfrac{17}{5}x^{\frac{1}{2}} \quad \Rightarrow \quad f'(x) = \dfrac{1}{2}\cdot\dfrac{17}{5}x^{\frac{1}{2}-\frac{2}{2}} = \dfrac{17}{10}x^{-\frac{1}{2}} = \dfrac{17}{10\sqrt{x}}$

u. $y(x)=\frac{\pi\sqrt{x}}{\sqrt{2}}=\frac{\pi}{\sqrt{2}}x^{\frac{1}{2}} \quad\Rightarrow\quad y'(x)=\frac{1}{2}\cdot\frac{\pi}{\sqrt{2}}x^{\frac{1}{2}-\frac{2}{2}}=\frac{\pi}{2\sqrt{2}}x^{-\frac{1}{2}}=\frac{\pi}{2\sqrt{2}\sqrt{x}}=$

$$=\frac{\pi}{2\sqrt{2x}}$$

v. $h(t)=-16t^2+35t+4 \quad\Rightarrow\quad h'(t)=2(-16)t^{2-1}+1\cdot 35t^{1-1}+0\cdot 4x^{0-1}$

$$=-32t+35$$

w. $y(z)=\sqrt[4]{z^3}=z^{\frac{3}{4}} \quad\Rightarrow\quad y'(z)=\frac{3}{4}z^{\frac{3}{4}-\frac{4}{4}}=\frac{3}{4}z^{-\frac{1}{4}}=\frac{3}{4x^{\frac{1}{4}}}=\frac{3}{4\sqrt[4]{x}}$

x. $f(x)=9x^7-\pi\sqrt[3]{x}+\frac{1}{\sqrt{x}}+x=9x^7-\pi x^{\frac{1}{3}}+x^{-\frac{1}{2}}+x$

$$\Rightarrow\quad f'(x)=7\cdot 9x^{7-1}-\left(\frac{1}{3}\right)\pi x^{\frac{1}{3}-\frac{3}{3}}+\left(-\frac{1}{2}\right)x^{-\frac{1}{2}-\frac{2}{2}}+1x^{1-1}=$$

$$=63x^6-\frac{\pi}{3}x^{-\frac{2}{3}}-\frac{1}{2}x^{-\frac{3}{2}}+1=63x^6-\frac{\pi}{3x^{\frac{2}{3}}}-\frac{1}{2x^{\frac{3}{2}}}+1=$$

$$=63x^6-\frac{\pi}{3\sqrt[3]{x^2}}-\frac{1}{2\sqrt{x^3}}+1$$

y. $f(x)=-8\sqrt[3]{x^5}+\frac{1}{\sqrt[5]{x^3}}+x^{\frac{2}{3}}=-8x^{\frac{5}{3}}+\frac{1}{x^{\frac{3}{5}}}+x^{\frac{2}{3}}=-8x^{\frac{5}{3}}+x^{-\frac{3}{5}}+x^{\frac{2}{3}}$

$$\Rightarrow\quad f'(x)=\frac{5}{3}(-8)x^{\frac{5}{3}-\frac{3}{3}}+\left[-\frac{3}{5}\right]x^{-\frac{3}{5}-\frac{5}{5}}+\left[\frac{2}{3}\right]x^{\frac{2}{3}-\frac{3}{3}}=-\frac{40}{3}x^{\frac{2}{3}}-\frac{3}{5}x^{-\frac{8}{5}}+\frac{2}{3}x^{-\frac{1}{3}}$$

$$=-\frac{40}{3}x^{\frac{2}{3}}-\frac{3}{5x^{\frac{8}{5}}}+\frac{2}{3x^{\frac{1}{3}}}=-\frac{40}{3}\sqrt[3]{x^2}-\frac{3}{5\sqrt[5]{x^8}}+\frac{2}{3\sqrt[3]{x}}$$

z. $y(x)=7r^{\pi} \quad\Rightarrow\quad y'(x)=\pi\cdot 7r^{\pi-1}=7\pi r^{\pi-1}$

aa. $y(x)=2r^{2.35} \quad\Rightarrow\quad y'(x)=2.35\cdot 2r^{2.35-1}=4.7r^{1.35}$

ab. $g(x)=-6x^{-6}+2x^{-\frac{2}{5}}+\frac{1}{x^{-\frac{1}{2}}}=-6x^{-6}+2x^{-\frac{2}{5}}+x^{\frac{1}{2}}$

$$\Rightarrow\quad g'(x)=-6(-6)x^{-6-1}+\left[-\frac{2}{5}\right]2x^{-\frac{2}{5}-\frac{5}{5}}+\frac{1}{2}x^{\frac{1}{2}-\frac{2}{2}}=36x^{-7}-\frac{4}{5}x^{-\frac{7}{5}}+\frac{1}{2}x^{-\frac{1}{2}}$$

$$=\frac{36}{x^7}-\frac{4}{5x^{\frac{7}{5}}}+\frac{1}{2x^{\frac{1}{2}}}=\frac{36}{x^7}-\frac{4}{5\sqrt[5]{x^7}}+\frac{1}{2\sqrt{x}}$$

ac. $y(x)=7x^{-5} \quad\Rightarrow\quad y'(x)=-5\cdot 7x^{-5-1}=-35x^{-6}=-\frac{35}{x^6}$

ad. $y(x)=\frac{7}{x^5}=7x^{-5} \quad\Rightarrow\quad y'(x)=-5\cdot 7x^{-5-1}=-35x^{-6}=-\frac{35}{x^6}$

ae. $f(x)=ax^{\text{n}} \quad\Rightarrow\quad f'(x)=n\cdot ax^{\text{n}-1}=anx^{\text{n}-1}$

CHAPTER 15 - DERIVATIVES AND THE PROBLEM OF CHANGE

ANSWERS TO THE STUDY QUESTIONS

1. If we take the derivative of Galileo's law of fall, what function do we get? What if we take the second derivative of Galileo's law of fall?

   The derivative of Galileo's law of fall is $d'(t) = 32t$. The derivative of this is $d''(t) = 32$.

2. What is acceleration?

   Acceleration is how fast the velocity is changing. In other words, acceleration is how fast an object speeds up or slows down.

3. Why are the units of acceleration ft/s^2 or m/s^2? In other words, why the odd phrase "second *squared*"?

   The units of acceleration are ft/s^2 or m/s^2. The real meaning of these units comes through when we say them in words, "feet per second per second." Feet per second is the unit for velocity, and the other "per second" tells us that the velocity is changing every second.

4. In terms of limits, what is the definition of instantaneous acceleration?

   In terms of limits, the definition of instantaneous acceleration is, $a(t) = v'(t) = \lim_{\Delta t \to 0}\left(\frac{\Delta v}{\Delta t}\right)$.

5. What is $\Delta v/\Delta t$?

   $\Delta v/\Delta t$ is average acceleration.

6. What are some different notations we can use to refer to instantaneous acceleration?

   Some different notations we can use to refer to instantaneous acceleration are $a(t) = d''(t) = \frac{d^2d}{dt^2} = v'(t) = \frac{dv}{dt}$.

7. Why did we add the negative sign to Galileo's law of fall?

   We added the negative sign to Galileo's law of fall to show that a dropped object is moving downwards.

8. Why doesn't the law of fall—even if we add the negative sign—tell us the distance above the ground, even though the law can give the distance that the object has fallen?

   The law of fall tells us how far an object has fallen but it can only tell us an object's distance above the ground once we know where the object was dropped from.

9. For the height function $h(t) = -16t^2 + 12$, how did we verify that the initial height of the object was 12 feet above the ground?

   For the function $h(t) = -16t^2 + 12$, we verified that the initial height of the object was 12 feet above the ground by plugging 0 seconds in for t.

10. From the function $h(t) = -16t^2 + 12$ can you tell how far the object has fallen after it has fallen for t seconds?

    From the function $h(t) = -16t^2 + 12$, you cannot tell how far the object has fallen after t seconds, at least not directly. Instead, this function tells us how far above the ground the object is after t seconds.

11. What physical aspect of the situation does each of the two terms in $h(t) = -16t^2 + 12$ represent? What units of measurement is each of the terms in?

    In the function $h(t) = -16t^2 + 12$, $-16t^2$ represents how far the object has fallen, and represents the initial height when the object was dropped. Each of the terms are measured in feet.

12. To what kinds of objects does $h(t) = -16t^2 + 12$ apply?

    The function $h(t) = -16t^2 + 12$ applies to any object at all, assuming that air resistance is so small that it can be ignored.

13. What does it mean to "interpret" mathematics?

    Numbers, by themselves, don't tell us much of anything. They need to be interpreted to have meaning. To understand what numbers are saying about

the world we need to know the numbers, what they represent, and the context in which they are operating. For example, we wouldn't know what $d(t) = 16t^2$ means except that we were told the context for this function (it describes a situation in which an object is dropped near the earth and air resistance can be ignored). We were told that represents the amount of time that has elapsed since the moment the object was dropped, and represents the distance the object has fallen in that time. Once we had all this information, we could interpret the function and its output.

14. What is the difference between pure and applied mathematics?

    Pure mathematics deals just with mathematical objects like numbers and functions, whereas applied mathematics deals with how math intersects with the real world.

15. What do Platonists believe about mathematics?

    Platonists believe that mathematical objects have an existence independent of any human mind.

16. What does the second term of height function $h(t) = -16t^2 + 35t + 4$ represent? In what units must each term be?

    The second term in the height function $h(t) = -16t^2 + 35t + 4$ is $35t$ and it takes into account the initial speed of the object. Since the function is finding the object's height in feet above the ground, each of the term's units must also be in feet.

17. What is the speed of an object thrown straight up in the air when it reaches its maximum height?

    When an object that is thrown straight up in the air reaches its maximum height its velocity is zero.

18. What is the equivalent of 32 ft/s^2 in m/s^2?

    The equivalent of 32 ft/s^2 in m/s^2 is $9.8 m/s^2$.

19. Consider the object whose height is given by $h(t) = -16t^2 + 35t + 4$ as before. What if we change the second term's sign to negative as follows: $h(t) = -16t^2 - 35t + 4$. What does that mean physically?

    If we make the second term in our height function negative, $h(t) = -16t^2 + 35t + 4$, then the initial speed of the object is the same as before but in the opposite direction. In this case, the object is thrown down at 35 ft/s from 4 feet above the ground and will speed up for a very short amount of time before it hits the ground.

20. What is the general free fall formula for height above the ground? What do the subscripts on the coefficients mean?

    The general free fall formula for height above the ground is $h(t) = -16t^2 + v_0t + h_0$. The subscripts on the coefficients show that we are talking about the initial velocity and the initial height, that is, the velocity and height of the object at $t = 0$ seconds.

21. What is the general form for the gravitational term (for any gravitational constant)?

    The general form for the gravitational term is $\frac{1}{2}gt^2$.

22. What is the sun's gravitational constant? What is the moon's?

    The sun's gravitational constant is 900 ft/s^2. The moon's gravitational constant is 5 ft/s^2.

23. What is the difference between describing and discovering, as we have discussed them in this chapter?

    The difference between describing and discovering in mathematics (as we have discussed in this chapter) is that describing is something we do after we make observations and experiments, whereas discovering is something we do without looking at the world; it is something that we can do with paper and a pencil, and yet it can still tell us truths about the physical world. In both cases, something miraculous is happening. In the case of describing, it is miraculous that complex change can often be described quite simply using math (e.g., $16t^2$). In the case of discovering, it is miraculous that scribbling on a piece of

paper, without reference to the physical world, can tell us new information about what really happens in the world (e.g., finding an object's instantaneous speed by taking the derivative of the free fall formula).

24. Can you discover the formula for the circumference of a circle from the formula of its area? Explain.

    You can discover the formula for the circumference of a circle from the formula of its area by taking the derivative of the formula for area. The formula for the area of a circle is $A(r) = \pi r^2$. Using the power rule, we find that the derivative of this is $A'(r) = 2\pi r$, which is also the formula for the circumference of a circle.

25. What is the most common explanation for the applicability of mathematics to the physical world? Why might someone find a purely evolutionary explanation implausible?

    The most common explanation for the applicability of mathematics to the physical world is that God made both humans and the universe. God designed humans in a way that they could know the world and he designed the world in a way that it could be known by humans. Someone might find a purely evolutionary explanation of the applicability of math implausible because evolution posits that our brains developed in such a way that we could better survive. It makes little sense then why our brains would be capable of discovering things that go beyond what we can even observe since these things clearly have nothing to do with our survival. According to the evolutionist then, we can discover truths about things that have nothing to do with survival using our brains which are hardwired for survival.

26. What are the three Pythagorean assumptions that made the Scientific Revolution—including calculus—possible?

    The three Pythagorean assumptions that made the Scientific Revolution possible are that the universe is ordered according to perfect mathematical laws, the divine reason is the organizer of nature, and that human reason can discern the divine pattern.

27. Who revived the Platonic-Pythagorean tradition during the Scientific Revolution?

    Galileo revived the Platonic-Pythagorean tradition during the Scientific Revolution.

28. What are the two main theories of contemporary physics?

    The two main theories of contemporary physics are general relativity and quantum mechanics.

29. How is mathematics like a seeing-eye dog?

    Mathematics is like a seeing-eye dog because it takes us where our senses cannot go.

30. How might mathematics be seen as evidence for God's existence?

    Mathematics can be seen as evidence for God's existence because the Pythagorean assumptions are a much more logically satisfying explanation for the applicability of mathematics than the evolutionist's explanation.

EXERCISE SOLUTIONS

1) a. $h(t) = -16\,t^2 + 4 \quad \Rightarrow \quad h(0) = -16(0)^2 + 4 = 4 \text{ ft}$

   b. $h(t) = -16t^2 + 100 \quad \Rightarrow \quad h(0) = -16(0) + 100 = 100 \text{ ft}$

   c. $h(t) = -16t^2 \quad \Rightarrow \quad h(0) = -16(0)^2 = 0 \text{ ft}$

   The object won't fall since it's already on the ground.

   d. The second term of these functions *is* the initial height.

2) a. $h(t) = -16t^2 + 4 \quad \Rightarrow \quad v(t) = h'(t) = -32t$

   $\Rightarrow \quad a(t) = v'(t) = h''(t) = -32$

   b. $h(t) = -16t^2 + 100 \quad \Rightarrow \quad v(t) = h'(t) = -32t$

   $\Rightarrow \quad a(t) = v'(t) = h''(t) = -32$

   c. $h(t) = -16t^2 \quad \Rightarrow \quad v(t) = h'(t) = -32t$

   $\Rightarrow \quad a(t) = v'(t) = h''(t) = -32$

3) a. $h(t) = -16t^2 + 4 \quad \Rightarrow \quad 0 = -16t^2 + 4 \quad \Rightarrow \quad 16t^2 = 4$

$\Rightarrow \quad t^2 = \frac{4}{16} = \frac{1}{4}$

$\Rightarrow \quad t = \pm\sqrt{\frac{1}{4}} = \pm\frac{1}{2} \quad \Rightarrow \quad t = .5$ s (We'll stick to only positive time.)

$\Rightarrow \quad v(t) = -32t \quad \Rightarrow \quad v(.5) = -32(.5) = -16 \quad \Rightarrow \quad v_{.5} = -16$ ft/s

b. $h(t) = -16t^2 + 100 \quad \Rightarrow \quad 0 = -16t^2 + 100 \quad \Rightarrow \quad 6t^2 = 100$

$\Rightarrow \quad t^2 = \frac{100}{16} = \frac{25}{4} \quad \Rightarrow$

$\Rightarrow \quad t = \pm\sqrt{\frac{25}{4}} = \pm\frac{5}{2} \quad \Rightarrow \quad t = 2.5$ s

$\Rightarrow \quad v(t) = -32t \quad \Rightarrow \quad v(.5) = -32(2.5) = -80 \quad \Rightarrow \quad v_{2.5} = -80$ ft/s

c. $h(t) = -16t^2 \quad \Rightarrow \quad 0 = -16t^2 \quad \Rightarrow \quad t = 0$ s

$\Rightarrow \quad v(0) = 32(0) = 0$ ft/s

4) $h(t) = -16t^2 + 65t + 6$

a. $v(t) = h'(t) = -32t + 65$

$a(t) = v'(t) = h''(t) = -32$

b. $t = 0 \quad \Rightarrow \quad h(0) = -16(0)^2 + 65(0) + 6 = 6$ ft

$v(0) = -32(0) + 65 = 65$ ft/s

c. Object is highest when $v = 0$

$\Rightarrow v(t) = 0 - 32t + 65 \quad \Rightarrow \quad 32t = 65 \quad \Rightarrow \quad t = \frac{65}{32} = 2.03$ s

$h(2.03) = -16(2.03)^2 + 65(2.03) + 6 =$

$= -16(4.13) + 132.0 + 6 =$

$= -66.08 + 132.0 + 6 =$

$= 71.9$ ft

5) $h(t) = -16t^2 + 200t + 6$

a. $v(t) = h'(t) = -32t + 200$

$a(t) = v'(t) = h''(t) = -32$

b. $h(0) = -16(0)^2 + 200(0) + 6 = 6$ ft

$v(0) = -32(0) + 200 = 200$ ft/s

c. $v = 0 = -32t + 200 \quad \Rightarrow \quad 32t = 200 \quad \Rightarrow \quad t = \frac{200}{32} = \frac{100}{16} = \frac{25}{4} = 6.25$ s

$h(6.25) = -16(6.25)^2 + 200(6.25) + 6$

$= -625 + 1250 + 6$

$= 631$ ft

6) $h(t) = -16t^2 - 4t + 12$

a. $v(t) = h'(t) = -32t - 4$

$a(t) = v'(t) = h''(t) = -32$

b. $h = 0 = -16t^2 - 4t + 12 \quad \Rightarrow \quad (-4t - 4)(4t - 3)$

$$\swarrow \quad \text{or} \quad \searrow$$

$$\begin{array}{ll} -4t - 4 = 0 & 4t - 3 = 0 \\ -4t = 4 & 4t = 3 \\ t = -1 & t = 3/4 \end{array}$$

$v(.75) = -32(.75) - 4 = -28$ ft/s

7) $h(t) = -16t^2 + v_{.0}t + h_0$

$v(t) = -32t + v_0$

$a(t) = -32$

CHAPTER 16 - GRAPHS AND SLOPES

ANSWERS TO THE STUDY QUESTIONS

1. Why are we looking at the graphs of derivatives?

   We are looking at the graphs of derivatives to better understand what is going on with derivatives. By looking at their graphs, we can actually "see" features of functions that are otherwise terribly abstract.

2. What is analytic geometry? When was it developed?

   Analytic geometry combines algebra (what is meant by *analytic*) and geometry, that is, it combines numbers with shapes, and it does so using the Cartesian coordinate system. Analytic geometry was developed in the early to mid-1600s.

3. What mathematical "realm" have we been looking at mostly up until now?

   Up until now, we have mostly been looking at the realm of numbers and we have largely ignored the realm of shapes.

4. Explain how formulas are actually sentences.

   Formulas are actually sentences which talk about numbers. We could write formulas in ordinary English, but they would be long and cumbersome, so instead we use symbols so that these sentences about numbers are more efficient and easier to understand.

5. How do Cartesian coordinates connect the two fundamental mathematical "realms"?

   In the Cartesian coordinate system, a two-number address is assigned to each and every point on a graph in the form of (x, y). A point is a geometrical object, and points can be combined to create other geometrical shapes, and since all

these points have numerical addresses, the two fundamental mathematical "realms" are connected.

6. What are two of the main shapes that will occupy much of our time in this book?

   The two main shapes that will occupy much of our time in this book are lines and parabolas.

7. How does the formula $y = 2x + 1$ (when interpreted as a line) refer to an infinite number of points?

   The formula $y = 2x + 1$ (when interpreted as a line) refers to an infinite number of points because, as we have seen, lines are made up of an infinite number of points. For every x-value that we plug into this function there is a unique y-value, which, geometrically speaking, means that for every point on the line, there is a unique two-digit (x, y) address. Since there are an infinite number of x-values to pick from, there are an infinite number of addresses or points on the line.

8. How does the formula $y = mx + b$ (when interpreted as a line) refer to an infinite number of lines?

   The formula $y = mx + b$ (when interpreted as a line) refers to an infinite number of lines because it is the general formula for a line, for any line whatsoever and so for *all of them*.

9. What do the m and b stand for geometrically in the formula $y = mx + b$?

   In the formula $y = mx + b$, the stands for the slope of the line, and b stands for the y-intercept, where the line crosses or intersects the y-axis.

10. Geometrically, what is the derivative of a function?

    Geometrically, the derivative of a function is the slope of that function.

11. In terms of the limit notation what is the definition of a derivative of a function $y(x)$?

    In terms of the limit notation, the definition of a derivative of a function $y(x)$ is $\lim_{\Delta x \to 0} \left(\frac{\Delta y}{\Delta x} \right)$.

12. Geometrically, what is the shape of the function $y(x) = x^2$?

    Geometrically, the shape of the function $y(x) = x^2$ is a parabola.

13. What are the four kinds of values that a slope can take? What do each of these mean in terms of "steepness"?

    The four kinds of values that a slope can take are negative, zero, positive, or undefined. A negative slope, when read from left to right, slopes downwards; a zero slope does not slope at all, it is a horizontal line; a positive slope goes upward; and an undefined slope is infinitely steep, it is a vertical line.

14. What is a secant line? Where do we get the word "secant"?

    A secant line is a line connecting two points on a parabola. We get the word "secant" from the Latin word *secare* which means "to cut." The secant line "cuts" the curve of a parabola.

15. Why do we talk about the slope*s* (plural) of a parabola?

    We talk about the slopes (plural) of a parabola because a parabola curves and so its steepness is constantly changing. This means that a parabola has a different slope at any given point, and so it has many different slopes.

16. What is a tangent line? Where do we get the word "tangent"?

    A tangent line is a line that touches—rather than cutting—the curve at only one point. The word "tangent" comes from the Latin word *tangere* which means "to touch."

17. What does the steepness of a line that's tangent to a point on a parabola show?

    The steepness of a line that's tangent to a point on a parabola shows the steepness or slope of the parabola at the point where it touches the parabola.

18. Why doesn't it make sense to talk about secant lines and tangent lines of a *straight line*?

    It doesn't make sense to talk about secant lines and tangent lines of a straight line because there are no secant or tangent lines of a straight line. There are no secant lines of a straight line because no line can cut the straight line at

just two points, and there are no tangent lines because there are no lines that can touch only a single point on the straight line and still have the same slope.

19. In terms of the delta notation what is the slope of the secant line?

    In terms of delta notation, the slope of the secant line is $\frac{\Delta y}{\Delta x}$.

20. In words—and in terms of a secant line and tangent line—what is a derivative?

    In words—and in terms of a secant line and tangent line—the derivative of $y(x)$ is the limit of the slope of the secant line as it approaches the slope of the tangent line.

21. Write out the symbolic definition of a derivative and label it in terms of the slope of a secant line and the slope of a tangent line.

    The symbolic definition of a derivative is $y' = \frac{dy}{dx} = \lim_{\Delta x \to 0}\left(\frac{\Delta y}{\Delta x}\right)$ where $\frac{dy}{dx}$ refers to the slope of the tangent line, and $\lim_{\Delta x \to 0}\left(\frac{\Delta y}{\Delta x}\right)$ refers to the slope of the secant line as Δx approaches 0.

CHAPTER 17 - SLOPES AND DERIVATIVES

ANSWERS TO THE STUDY QUESTIONS

1. In words—and in terms of a secant line and tangent line—what is a derivative?

   In words—and in terms of a secant line and tangent line—the derivative of $y(x)$ is the limit of the slope of the secant line as it approaches the slope of the tangent line.

2. Write out the symbolic definition of a derivative and label it in terms of the slope of a secant line and the slope of a tangent line.

   The symbolic definition of a derivative is $y' = \frac{dy}{dx} = \lim_{\Delta x \to 0}\left(\frac{\Delta y}{\Delta x}\right)$ where $\frac{dy}{dx}$ refers to the slope of the tangent line, and $\lim_{\Delta x \to 0}\left(\frac{\Delta y}{\Delta x}\right)$ refers to the slope of the secant line as Δx approaches 0.

3. What are the two basic steps in the Method of Increments in terms of secant and tangent lines?

   In terms of secant and tangent lines, the two basic steps in the Method of Increments are finding the slope of the secant line and then finding the slope of the tangent line.

4. We relabeled the graph from the previous chapter to put it in terms more closely matching our Method of Increments.

   a. How did we relabel point A?
   b. How did we relabel point B?

   a. We relabeled point A with the generic address (y, x).
   b. We relabeled point B with the address $(x + \Delta x, y + \Delta y)$.

5. Using a straightedge, neatly draw and label Figure 17.3 from the chapter (the figure where we put the graph in terms of our Method of Increments). What is the formula for $\Delta y/\Delta x$? Geometrically, what does $\Delta y/\Delta x$ represent?

See figure 17.3 for the drawing. The generic formula for $\frac{\Delta y}{\Delta x}$ is $\frac{y(x+\Delta x)-y(x)}{\Delta x}$. Evaluated at $x = 3$, the formula for $\frac{\Delta y}{\Delta x}$ is $6 + \Delta x$. Geometrically, $\frac{\Delta y}{\Delta x}$ represents the slope of the line between two points, that is, the slope of the secant line.

6. Fill in the following:

   The slope of $y(x)$ at point (x, y) = slope of $y(x)$'s ________________ at point (x, y).

   The slope of $y(x)$ at point (x, y) = slope of $y(x)$'s tangent line at point (x, y).

7. Fill in the following:

   The slope of $y(x)$'s ___________ line at (x, y) = limit of the slope of $y(x)$'s ___________ line between the two points (x, y) and $(x+\Delta x, y+\Delta y)$ as Δx approaches 0.

   The slope $y(x)$'s tangent line at (x, y) = limit of the slope of 's secant line between the two points (x, y) and $(x+\Delta x, y+\Delta y)$ as Δx approaches 0.

8. In symbols, what is the *average* slope?

   In symbols, the average slope is $\frac{\Delta y}{\Delta x}$.

9. In symbols, what is the *instantaneous* slope? What does *instantaneous* mean if we're not talking about time?

   In symbols, the instantaneous slope is $\frac{dy}{dx}$. "Instantaneous" does not necessarily indicate an instant in time but the instantaneous rate of change of y with respect to x.

10. Geometrically, what does $\Delta y/\Delta x$ mean?

    Geometrically, $\frac{\Delta y}{\Delta x}$ is the secant line of a function.

11. Geometrically, what does dy/dx mean?

    Geometrically, $\frac{dy}{dx}$ is the tangent line of a function.

12. Geometrically, what does the Power Rule help us find?

    Geometrically, the Power Rule helps us find the slope of a function's tangent line.

13. What problem are we ultimately interested in here?

    The problem we are ultimately interested in is the problem of change and how calculus fits into Western civilization's ongoing quest to solve it.

EXERCISE SOLUTIONS

1) $y(x) = x^2$ (approaching $x = 3$ from values *less than* 3)

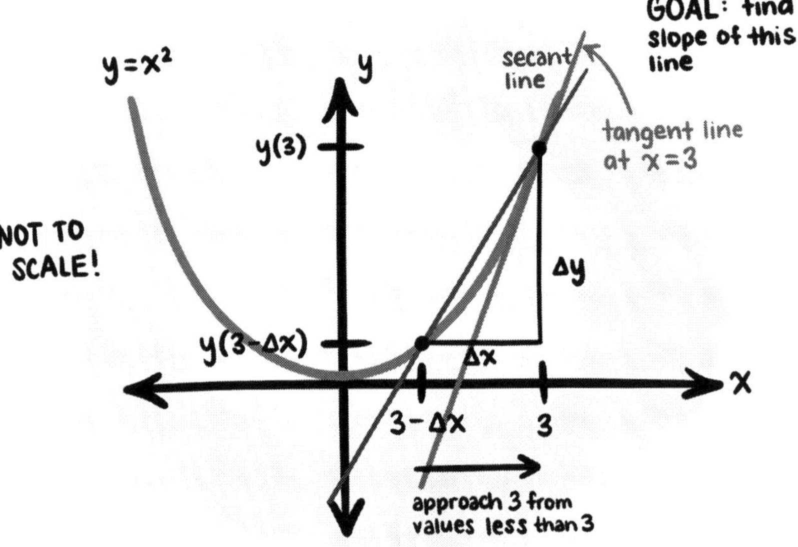

$$\frac{\Delta y}{\Delta x} = \frac{y(3) - y(3-\Delta x)}{\Delta x}$$
$$= \frac{3^2 - (3-\Delta x)^2}{\Delta x} = \frac{9-(3-\Delta x)(3-\Delta x)}{\Delta x} = \frac{9-(9-3\Delta x - 3\Delta x + (\Delta x)^2)}{\Delta x}$$
$$= \frac{9-9+6\Delta x - (\Delta x)^2}{\Delta x} = \frac{6\Delta x - (\Delta x)^2}{\Delta x} = 6 - \Delta x \qquad (\Delta x \neq 0)$$

The slope (at $x = 3$) $= \left.\frac{dy}{dx}\right|_{x=3} = \lim_{\Delta x \to 0}(6 - \Delta x) = 6 = \frac{6}{1}$

2) $y(x) = x^2$

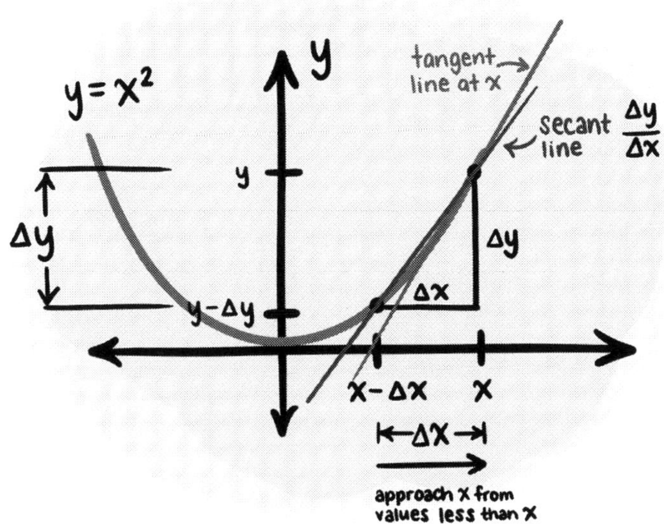

$$
\begin{aligned}
\frac{\Delta y}{\Delta x} &= \frac{y(x) - y(x-\Delta x)}{\Delta x} \\
&= \frac{x^2 - (x-\Delta x)^2}{\Delta x} \\
&= \frac{x^2 - (x-\Delta x)(x-\Delta x)}{\Delta x} \\
&= \frac{x^2 - (x^2 - 2x\Delta x + (\Delta x)^2)}{\Delta x} \\
&= \frac{x^2 - x^2 + 2x\Delta x - (\Delta x)^2}{\Delta x} = \frac{2x\Delta x - (\Delta x)^2}{\Delta x} = 2x - \Delta x \qquad (\Delta x \neq 0)
\end{aligned}
$$

$$\text{Slope} = y'(x)\ \frac{dy}{dx} = \lim_{\Delta x \to 0}(2x - \Delta x) = 2x$$

$$\left.\frac{dy}{dx}\right|_{x=1} = y'(2) = 2(1) = 2$$

$$\left.\frac{dy}{dx}\right|_{x=-1} = y'(-1) = 2(-1) = -2$$

$$\left.\frac{dy}{dx}\right|_{x=5} = y'(5) = 2(5) = 10$$

3) $y(t) = -16t^2 \qquad \dfrac{dy}{dt} = 2\cdot(-16)t^{2-1} = -32t = y'(t)$

$$\left.\frac{dy}{dt}\right|_{t=0} = -32(0) = 0$$

$$\left.\frac{dy}{dt}\right|_{t=2} = -32(2) = -64$$

$$\left.\frac{dy}{dt}\right|_{t=8} = -32(8) = -256$$

4) $\dfrac{\Delta f}{\Delta x} = \dfrac{f(c+h) - f(c)}{h} \quad \Rightarrow \quad f'(x) = \lim\limits_{h\to 0}\dfrac{f(c+h) - f(c)}{h}$

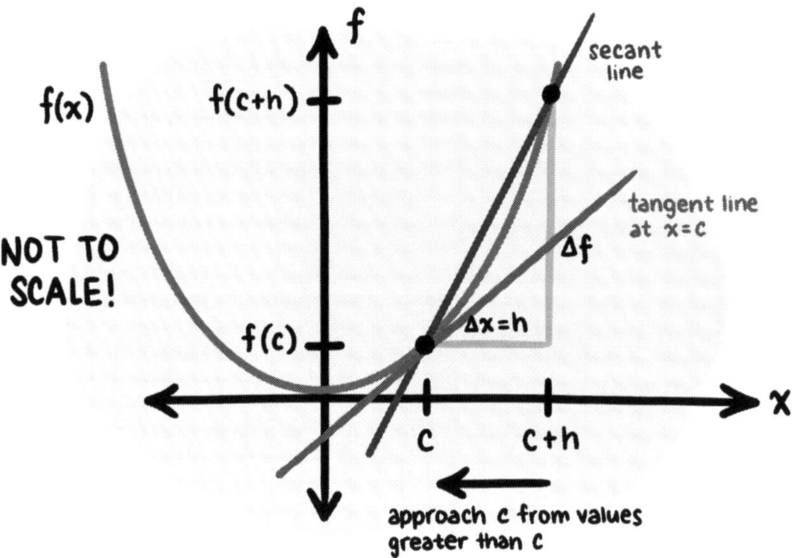

5) $y(x) = 5x^{15} + 17x^{10} + 11 \qquad \Rightarrow$

$$y'(x) = 15.5x^{15-1} + 10\cdot 17x^{10-1} + 0$$

$$= 75x^{14} + 170x^9 \qquad \Rightarrow$$

$$y'(1) = \left.\frac{dy}{dx}\right|_{x=1} = 75(1)^{14} + 170(1)^9 = 245 = \frac{245}{1}$$

6) $h(t) = -16t^2 + 55t + 6 \quad \Rightarrow$

$$h'(t) = \frac{dh}{dt} = -32t + 55 \quad \Rightarrow$$

$$h'(0) = -32(0) + 55 = 55 = \frac{55}{1}$$

$$h'(1) = -32(1) + 55 = 23 = \frac{23}{1}$$

$$h'(6) = -32(6) + 55 = -137 = -\frac{137}{1}$$

7) $\dfrac{\Delta y}{\Delta x} = \dfrac{y(x + \Delta x) - y(x)}{\Delta x} =$ slope of the secant line

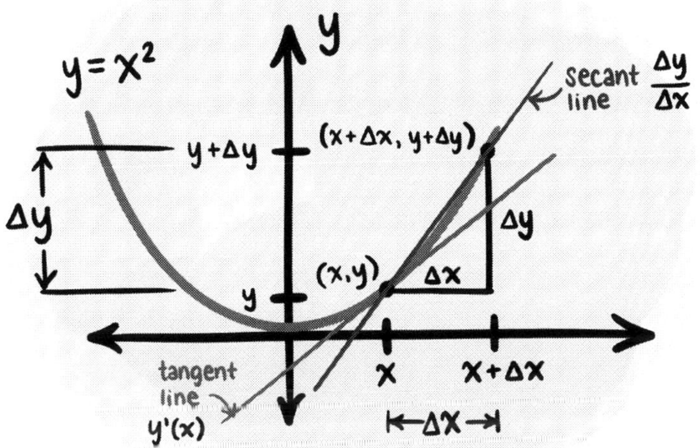

CHAPTER 18 - SLOPES AND THE PROBLEM OF CHANGE

ANSWERS TO THE STUDY QUESTIONS

1. Very briefly, what did we do in the previous two chapters? What are we going to do in this chapter?

   In the previous two chapters, we learned more about derivatives by looking at some of their features geometrically on a Cartesian coordinate system. We learned that the derivative of a function is the function's slope. In this chapter, we return to the problem of change, applying what we've learned to the physical phenomenon of free fall.

2. What is free fall?

   Free fall is the physical phenomenon when the only force acting upon an object is the force of gravity.

3. Write out Galileo's free fall in the form that gives distance fallen as a function of time.

   Galileo's law of free fall that gives distance as a function of time is $d(t) = 16t^2$.

4. Draw the physical picture and label it (but not from memory yet) as we did in the chapter. I suggest that you first draw the falling object (in this case a ball) and label the two "endpoints," t and $t + \Delta t$. Then label everything else. Use a straightedge.

   See figure 18.1a (the right-hand side of the graphic).

5. Draw the mathematical picture and label it (but not from memory yet) as we did in the chapter. I suggest you first draw the Cartesian coordinate, then curve for $d(t) = 16t^2$, then the two points on the curve. Add the labels from there. Use a straightedge.

   See figure 18.1a (the left-hand side of the graphic).

6. In the mathematical picture, why should we ignore everything less than $t = 0$?

In the mathematical picture, we should ignore everything less than $t = 0$, because the ball was dropped at $t = 0$, and therefore everything before that in the mathematical picture is physically meaningless.

7. If you were actually looking at the object in free fall what path would you see it follow, the mathematical path of the parabola or a straight line? Explain.

   A dropped object in free fall will follow the path of a straight line. The parabola is not the physical picture but the mathematical one and shows how the object's distance changes with time.

8. Write out, in symbols, the formula for instantaneous velocity in the case where the distance traveled is given by $d(t)$.

   The formula for instantaneous velocity in the case where distance traveled is given by $d(t)$ is $\lim_{\Delta t \to 0} \frac{\Delta d}{\Delta t}$.

9. If $d(t)$ is the distance an object travels during time t, what does the symbol $\Delta d/\Delta t$ represent? How is this related to the secant line between points t and $t + \Delta t$?

   When $d(t)$ is the distance an object travels during time t, $\frac{\Delta d}{\Delta t}$ represents the average speed over the interval Δt. It is equal to the slope of the secant line between points t and $t + \Delta t$.

10. Again, draw the mathematical picture (i.e., the curve of $d(t)=16t^2$) and draw the line that represents the average velocity. Use a straightedge.

    See figure 18.2a.

11. If $d(t)$ is the distance an object travels during time t, what does the following represent?

    $$\lim_{\Delta t \to 0} \frac{\Delta d}{\Delta t}$$

    How is this related to the tangent line at t?

    When $d(t)$ is the distance an object travels during time t, $\lim_{\Delta t \to 0} \frac{\Delta d}{\Delta t}$ represents the instantaneous speed. It is also the slope of the tangent line at t.

12. Again, draw the mathematical picture (i.e., the curve of $d(t)$=$16t^2$), label the two points, and then draw the line that represents the instantaneous velocity. Use a straightedge.

    See figure 18.2b.

13. In terms of a slope, what is the average speed? The instantaneous speed?

    In terms of slope, the average speed is the slope of the secant line, and the instantaneous speed is the slope of the tangent line.

14. Does the slope of $v(t)$ give the object's speed? Explain.

    The slope of $v(t)$ does not give the object's speed. You can find the object's speed by plugging into $v(t)$ the value of you're interested in. Instead, the slope of $v(t)$ gives us something else: acceleration.

15. Using the Power Rule, find $v(t)$ if $d(t)$=$16t^2$.

    We can find $v(t)$ by calculating the derivative of $d(t)$ using the Power Rule. The power rule says that for any power function of the form $f(x) = Kx^n$ its derivative is $f'(x) = nKx^{n-1}$. Since the power function we are dealing with is $d(t)$=$16t^2$, we know that f is d, x is t, n is 2, and K is 16. Plugging those values in to find the derivative we get $d'(t) = (2)(16)t^{2-1}$. So, the derivative of $d(t) = 16t^2$ is $v(t) = 32t$.

16. Draw the graph for $v(t) = 32t$ (not from memory), labeling both the average and instantaneous acceleration. Use a straightedge.

    See figure 18.3.

17. Using the limit notation, what is the definition of acceleration if the speed function is $v(t)$?

    If the speed function is $v(t)$, the definition of acceleration using the limit notation is $\lim_{\Delta t \to 0} \frac{\Delta v}{\Delta t}$.

18. What does $\Delta v/\Delta t$ represent?

    $\frac{\Delta v}{\Delta t}$ represents the average acceleration over the time interval Δt.

19. For $v(t) = 32t$, why is the line represented by $v(t)$ also the "secant" *and* "tangent" lines? What does this mean physically, in terms of speed and acceleration?

    The line that we get when we graph $v(t) = 32t$ is equal to the secant and tangent lines because the secant line is formed by taking two points on the graph and connecting them with a straight line, but the graph is already a straight line; and the tangent is formed by taking a point on the graph and drawing a line from that point with the slope of the graph at that point, but since the slope of the graph does not change, the tangent line will also fall exactly on the existing line. Physically, this means that the speed is changing at a constant rate, or, we could say, that acceleration is not changing at all.

20. Why is the following true?

$$\frac{\Delta v}{\Delta t} = \lim_{\Delta t \to 0} \frac{\Delta v}{\Delta t}$$

    is true because we are talking about a specific scenario where an object's acceleration is not changing. Since the object is speeding up at the same rate the entire time, it does not matter whether you choose to observe an instant in time or an interval of time, the rate of change will be the same. It is like a car travelling at a constant rate of 50 miles per hour. Over an hour, the vehicle's average speed was 50 miles per hour, but also, since the speed never changed, at any given moment, the vehicle's instantaneous speed was also 50 miles per hour. The difference here is that we are talking about acceleration and not speed.

21. Draw the graph for $a(t) = 32$ (not from memory).

    See figure 18.4.

22. Are most moving objects' accelerations constant?

    Most moving object's accelerations are not constant.

EXERCISE SOLUTIONS

See the relevant diagrams in the chapter.

CHAPTER 19 - MORE INFORMATION FROM DERIVATIVES AND THEIR GRAPHS

ANSWERS TO THE STUDY QUESTIONS

1. What is the difference between the derivative at a specific point and simply "the derivative"?

   The difference between the derivative at a specific point and simply "the derivative" is that the derivative at a specific point is a single numerical value, whereas "the derivative" of a function is itself a function which can help us find the derivative at a specific point.

2. Using a straightedge, draw the graphs for both $y(x) = x^2$ and its derivative $y'(x)=2x$. You need not draw them to scale; simply copy them from the diagram in the text.

   a. Calculate and label the functions' values for $y(x)$ and $y'(x)$ when $x = ½$.
   b. What does the value $y'(½)$ tell you about the original function, $y(x)$?
   c. Draw the tangent line to $y(x)$ at $x = ½$. Indicate its slope.

   See figure 19.1a.

   a. **When we plug in ½ for x into the original function we get $y\left(\frac{1}{2}\right)=\left(\frac{1}{2}\right)^2=\frac{1}{4}$. When we plug in the same value of x into the derivative we get $y'\left(\frac{1}{2}\right)=2\left(\frac{1}{2}\right)=1$.**
   b. **The value of $y'(½)$ tells us that the slope of the function $y(x)$ at $x(½)$ is 1.**
   c. **See the left-hand graphic of figure 19.1c.**

3. Fill in the blanks:

   value of $y'(x)$ = ____________________

   value of $y'(x) \neq$ ____________________

   Value of $y'(x)$ slope of $y(x)$. Value of $y'(x) \neq$ slope of $y'(x)$.

4. On the graphs you drew for study question (2),

   a. Calculate and label the functions' *values* for $y(x)$ and $y'(x)$ when $x = -½$.
   b. What does the value $y'(-½)$ tell you about the original function, $y(x)$?
   c. Draw the tangent line to $y(x)$ at $x = -½$.

   a. **When we plug in -½ for x into the original function we get $y\left(-\frac{1}{2}\right)=\left(-\frac{1}{2}\right)^2=\frac{1}{4}$. When we plug in the same value of x into the derivative we get $y'\left(-\frac{1}{2}\right)=2\left(-\frac{1}{2}\right)=-1$.**

   b. **The value of $y'(-½)$ tells us that the slope of the function $y(x)$ at $x=-½$ is -1.**

   c. **See the left-hand graphic of figure 19.1d.**

5. Draw the graph of $y'(x) = 2x$ by itself.

   a. What does the simple fact that all the output values of the function to the right of the vertical axis are positive tell you about the rough shape of $y(x)$ to the right of the vertical axis?
   b. What does the simple fact that all the output values of the function to the left of the vertical axis are negative tell you about the rough shape of $y(x)$ to the left of the vertical axis?
   c. What does the simple fact that the output value of the function at $x = 0$ is 0 tell you about the rough shape of $y(x)$ at $x=0$?
   d. What can you determine about $y(x)$ from the fact that the values of $y'(x)=2x$ in the upper right-hand corner are not only positive but also increase in value from left to right?
   e. What can you determine about $y(x)$ from the fact that the values of $y'(x)=2x$ in the lower left-hand corner are not only negative but also increase in value from left to right? Think in terms of absolute values.
   f. What does the simple fact that the function $y'(x)=2x$ is 0 at $x = 0$ tell you about the rough shape of $y(x)$ at $x=0$? (This is kind of a trick question.)

   See figure 19.1e.

   a. **The fact that all the output values of the function to the right of the vertical axis are positive tells us that the slope of the original function, $y(x)$,** to the right of the vertical axis is positive and therefore slanted upward toward the right.

b. The fact that all the output values of the function to the left of the vertical axis are negative tells us that the slope of the original function, $y(x)$, to the left of the vertical axis is negative and therefore slanted downward as we move toward the right.

c. The fact that the output value of the function at $x=0$ is 0 tells us that the slope of the original function, $y(x)$, is 0, or horizontal at $x=0$.

d. Since the values of $y'(x)=2x$ are positive and increasing in the upper right-hand corner, we can determine that the slope of the original function to the right of the vertical axis gets steeper and steeper in the positive direction.

e. Since the values of $y'(x)=2x$ are negative and increasing in the lower left-hand corner, we can determine that the slope of the original function to the left of the vertical axis gets less steep in the negative direction, that is, the slope is getting flatter. (recall that we are reading the graph from left to right).

f. The fact that the function $y'(x)=2x$ is 0 at $x=0$ tells us that the slope of $y(x)$ at $x=0$ is also 0 .

6. What is the absolute value of three? That is, what is $|3|$?

   The absolute value of 3 is 3 .

7. What is the absolute value of negative three? That is, what is $|-3|$?

   The absolute value of -3 is 3.

8. Write out the two rules for how absolute values relate to the steepness of slopes.

   a. If the absolute value of the derivative is getting larger, then the slope of the original function is getting steeper.

   b. If the absolute value of the derivative is getting smaller, then the slope of the original function is getting flatter.

9. Write out the two rules for how positive and negative values relate to the steepness of slopes.

a. **If the value of the derivative is positive, then the slope of the original function is sloping upward as we travel along the graph from left to right.**

b. **If the value of the derivative is *negative*, then the slope of the original function is sloping *downward* as we travel along the graph from left to right.**

10. Draw the graph of $y''(x) = 2$ by itself. The entire function $y''(x) = 2$ is flat. What does this say about the function $y'(x) = 2x$?

    See the right-hand graphic of figure 19.3a. Since the entire function $y''(x) = 2$ is flat, we know that the slope of the function it was derived from, $y'(x)$, is constant.

11. Draw the graph of $y'''(x) = 0$ by itself. The entire function $y'''(x) = 0$ is flat. What does this say about the function $y''(x) = 2$?

    See the green line in figure 19.3b. Since $y'''(x) = 0$ is flat and all output values are zero, we know that the slope of the function it was derived from, $y''(x)$, is 0, that is, flat.

EXERCISE SOLUTIONS

1) a. Since the *values* of $y' = 3x$ are negative for $x < 0$, the *slope* of y (the original function) is negative for values of $x < 0$, that is, y slopes downward (when moving from left to right, as usual).

   Since the *value* of $y' = 3x$ is 0 when $x = 0$, the *slope* of y (the original function) is 0 at $x = 0$, that is, y is flat exactly at $x = 0$.

   Since the *values* of $y' = 3x$ are positive for $x > 0$, the *slope* of y (the original function) is positive for values of $x > 0$, that is, y slopes upward (when moving from left to right).

   b. At $x = 0$ the slope of $y(x)$ flattens out, increasing in steepness from there, as x-values increase and move away from 0.

   c. As x-values approach 0 from the left, the *absolute* values of the derivative $y = 3x$ decrease, meaning that the slope of $y(x)$ gets less steep or flatter.

2) a. Since the value of $y' = 10$ is constant and positive, we know that the slope of the original function, $y(x)$, has a constant slope upwards *everywhere*. That means that $y(x)$ is a line that slopes upward; but we don't know where it crosses the y-axis just from the derivative.

b. The slope of $y(x)$ stays constant.

c. The slope of $y(x)$ stays constant.

3) a. Since the *values* of $y' = x$ are positive for $x < 0$, the slope of y (the original function) is positive for values of $x < 0$, that is, y slopes upward (when moving from left to right).

Since the *value* of $y' = x$ is 0 when $x = 0$, the slope of y (the original function) is 0 at $x = 0$, that is, y is flat exactly at $x = 0$.

Since the *values* of $y' = x$ are negative for $x > 0$, the slope of y (the original function) is negative for values of $x > 0$, that is, y slopes downward (when moving from left to right).

b. As x-values move away from 0 to the right, the *absolute* values of the derivative $y' = -x$ increase, meaning that the slope of $y(x)$ gets steeper (even though it is a downward slope).

c. As x-values approach 0 from the left, the values of the derivative $y' = -x$ decrease, meaning that the slope of $y(x)$ gets less steep or flatter.

4) a. Since the *values* of $y' = x^2$ are positive for $x < 0$, the *slope* of y (the original function) is positive for values of $x < 0$, that is, y slopes upward (when moving from left to right).

Since the *value* of $y' = x^2$ is 0 when $x = 0$, the *slope* of y (the original function) is 0 at $x = 0$, that is, y is flat exactly at $x = 0$.

Since the *values* of $y' = x^2$ are positive for $x > 0$, the *slope* of y (the original function) is positive for values of $x > 0$, that is, y slopes upward (when moving from left to right).

b. As x-values move away from 0 to the right, the values of the derivative $y' = x^2$ increase, meaning that the slope of $y(x)$ gets steeper.

c. As x-values approach 0 from the left, the values of the derivative $y' = x^2$ decrease, meaning that the slope of $y(x)$ gets less steep or flatter.

CHAPTER 20 - LOOKING CLOSER AT GRAPHS OF FREE FALL

ANSWERS TO THE STUDY QUESTIONS

1. What did we do in the last chapter?

   In the last chapter we learned how to interpret slopes of graphs in order to extract information about how a function behaves simply by looking at the graph of its derivative.

2. A function's derivative describes the behavior of the function's ___________.

   A function's derivative describes the behavior of the function's slope.

3. How is a derivative like a crystal ball? What does this have to do with the physical world?

   A derivative is like a crystal ball because we can look at the graph of a function's derivative and tell something about how the original function behaves. By looking at the graphs of derivatives that describe the physical world, we can predict how the world behaves, how it changes.

4. In the formula $d = 16t^2$, do d and t stand for numbers or physical properties? Explain.

   In the formula $d = 16t^2$, d and t stand for numbers and those numbers in turn stand for the physical properties of distance and time.

5. What is a good interpretation for "analytic" in the phrase "analytic geometry"?

   A good interpretation for "analytic" in the phrase "analytic geometry" is "algebraic."

6. What is the shape of the graph representing $d = 16t^{2?}$

   The shape of the graph representing $d = 16t^2$ is a parabola.

7. For the graph of Galileo's fall, what happens at $t < 0$?

For the graph of Galileo's law of free fall, any time less than 0 is meaningless. The graph does not tell us anything about what happens before an object is dropped at $t = 0$.

8. Which of the two graphs is the correct physical representation of $d = 16t^2$?

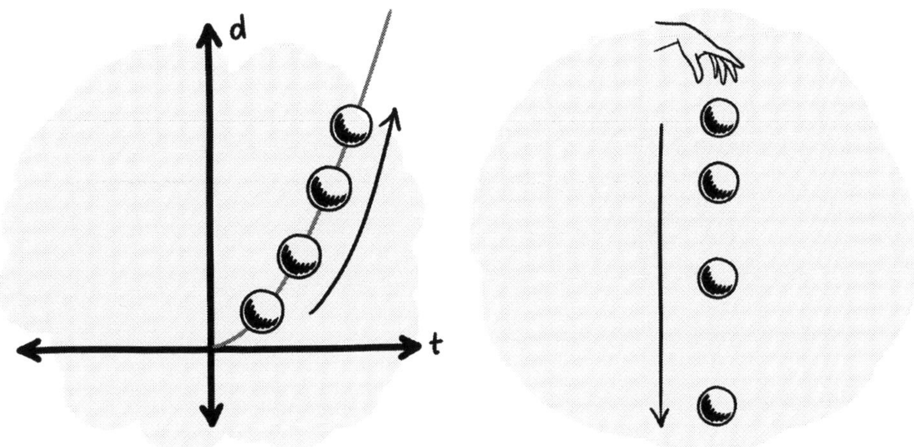

The correct physical representation of $d = 16t^2$ is the graph on the right.

9. Why did we add the negative sign to Galileo's law of fall?

We added the negative sign to Galileo's law of fall to account for the direction of the fall (i.e. downwards).

10. Describe the physical situation of the following free fall formula:

$$h(t) = -16t^2 + 30t + 5$$

The physical situation of the formula $h(t) = -16t^2 + 30t + 5$ is this: an object is dropped from 80 feet above the ground.

11. For the following $h(t)$ graph,

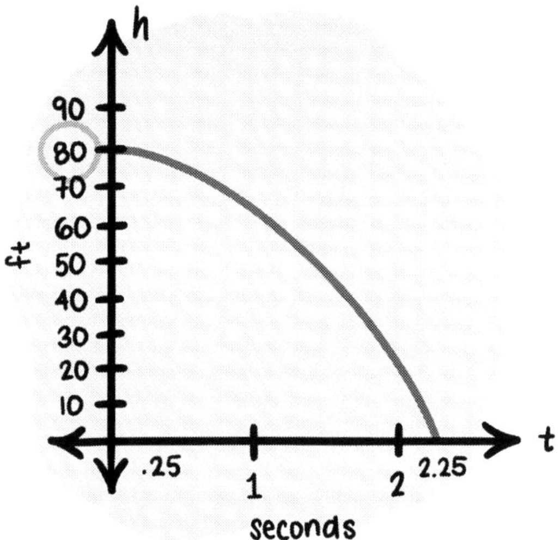

a. What does the 80 mean?

80 stands for the height in feet above the ground from which the object is dropped.

b. What are the units of measurement here?

The units of measurement on the y-axis are in feet, and the units of measurement on the x-axis are in seconds.

c. Is the object following a parabolic trajectory in the physical world? Explain.

The object is not following a parabolic trajectory in the physical world. Since the object is simply being dropped, the physical path would be straight down.

d. The slope of the graph at $t = 0$ is flat. What does this mean physically?

Since the slope of the graph at $t = 0$ is flat, we know that the object's speed is 0 at that moment in time.

e. Other than at $t = 0$, the slope is negative and therefore the speed of the falling object is negative. What does a negative speed mean in this case?

In this case, negative speed means that the object is moving downward.

f. After $t = 0$, the slope becomes steeper and steeper. What does this tell us about the object's speed? In other words, steeper means faster.

12. What is the general shape of the graph representing $v = -32t$?

The general shape of the graph representing $v = -32t$ is a straight line with a negative slope.

13. Answer the questions for the following velocity graph:

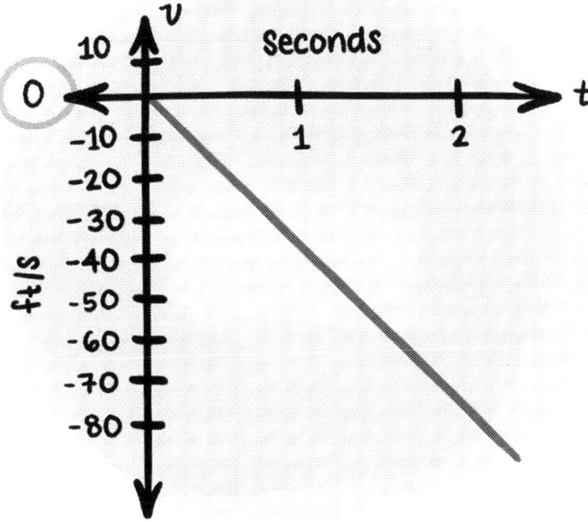

a. What are the units of measurement?

The units of measurement on the y-axis are in feet per second, and the units of measurement on the x-axis are in seconds.

b. What does the zero indicate here about the motion of the physical object? What does it indicate about the graph of the height function?

Since this is a graph of the object's speed over time, the zero indicates that the object's speed is 0 at $t = 0$. This also tells us that the slope of the height function at $t = 0$ is 0 or horizontal.

c. What information is the value of each point on the line giving us?

Each point on the line tells us the speed of the object at a given time, and it also tells us the slope of the height function at the corresponding time.

d. After t = 0, all the values of v(t) are negative. What does this tell us physically? What does it tell us mathematically about the graph of $h(t)$?

Since all the values of $v(t)$ are negative after $t = 0$, this tells us that in the physical scenario, the speed of the object is negative, or in the downward direction. It also tells us that the slope of the height function is negative, that is, it slopes downward.

e. The absolute values of $v(t)$ are increasing. What does this tell us physically? What does it tell us mathematically about the graph of $h(t)$?

Since the absolute values of $v(t)$ are increasing, we know that the speed of the object is increasing. It also tells us that the slope of the height function is getting steeper.

f. What does the constant slope of $v(t)$ tell us about acceleration?

Since the slope of $v(t)$ is constant, we know that the speed is changing at a constant rate, which means that the object's acceleration is constant.

g. What does the constant negative slope of $v(t)$ tell us about acceleration's graph?

Since we know that the slope of $v(t)$ is constant and negative, we know that the graph of the object's acceleration will be constant and negative which means it will be a flat line somewhere below the horizontal axis.

14. Suppose we have defined upward as positive and downward as negative, as usual. Can an object with a negative acceleration be moving upward? What does it mean for an object to have a negative acceleration?

An object with a negative acceleration can be moving upward. We know from experience that gravity always pulls objects in the downward direction. When something is thrown up into the air, gravity begins pulling it down even when the object is moving upward. We can tell when the object is going up that it slows down before it begins falling back to the ground. So even when an object is moving upward, it can experience a pull, or negative acceleration due to gravity.

15. What is Newton's second law and what two important physical properties does it connect to one another?

    Newton's second law is $F = ma$. This law demonstrates Newton's discovery that two important physical forces were closely connected: acceleration and force. We can translate talk of force into talk of acceleration.

16. Answer the questions for the following acceleration graph:

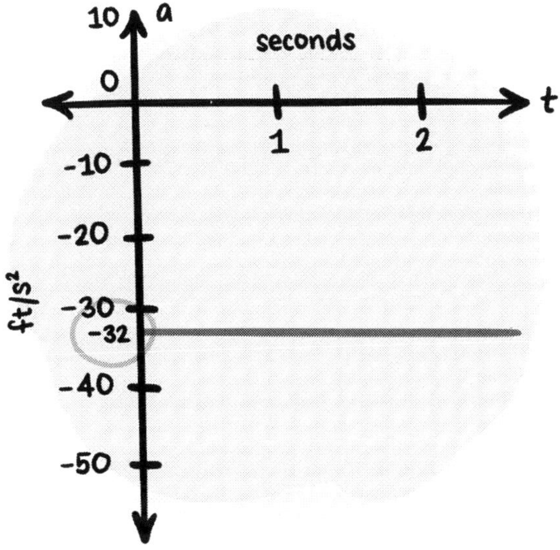

a. What are the units of measurement?

   The units of measurement on the y-axis are in feet per second per second (ft/s2), and the units of measurement on the x-axis are in seconds.

b. What information is the value of each point on the line giving us?

   Each point on the line is telling us what the acceleration of the object is at that moment. It is also telling us the slope of the function $v(t)$ at a given moment. Since $v(t)$ was a straight line, its slope was constant. So the output value of the function $a(t)$ is always -32 because the slope of $v(t)$ does not change, and because the acceleration due to gravity does not change.

c. All the values of $a(t)$ are *negative*. What does this tell us physically? What does it tell us mathematically about the graph of $v(t)$?

Since all the values of $a(t)$ are negative, we know that the object is always accelerating downward, which from experience we know is the case with gravity. We can also tell from this that the graph of $v(t)$ will be sloping downward.

d. The values of $a(t)$ are *constant*. What does this tell us physically? What does it tell us mathematically about the graph of $v(t)$?

Since the values of $a(t)$ are constant, we know that the object is always accelerating at the same rate. This also tells us that the graph of $v(t)$ will be a straight line.

17. Answer the questions for the following graph:

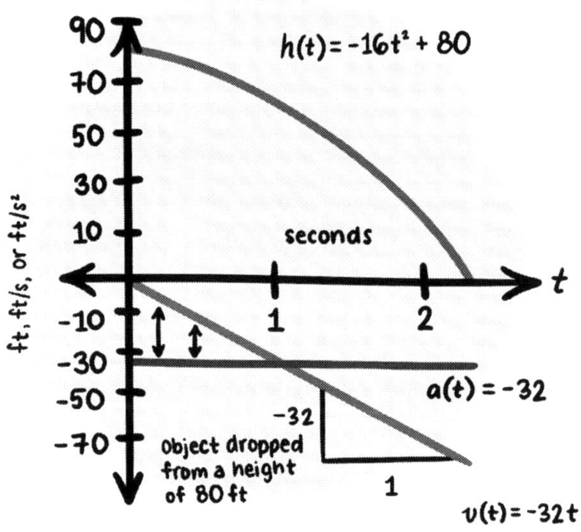

a. What are the units of measurement?

The units of measurement on the y-axis are in feet, feet per second, and feet per second per second (ft, ft/s, and ft/s2). $h(t)$ is measured in feet, $v(t)$ is measured in ft/s, and $a(t)$ is measured in ft/s2. The units of measurement on the x-axis are in seconds.

b. What is the slope of $h(t)$ at $t = 0$ and the value of $v(t)$ at $t = 0$? That is, what is the slope at $h(0)$ and the value of $v(0)$?

The slope at $h(0)$ is 0 and the value at $v(0)$ is also 0. The slope of $h(t)$ will always be the same as the value of $v(t)$ because the derivative tells us about the original function's slope, and $v(t)$ is the derivative of $h(t)$.

c. For $t>0$, the values of $v(t)$ are always negative. What does this tell you about the slope of $h(t)$ for $t>0$?

Since the values of $v(t)$ are negative for $t>0$, we know that the slope of $h(t)$ will also be negative for $t>0$.

d. For $t>0$, the absolute values of $v(t)$ are always increasing. What does this tell you about the slope of $h(t)$ for $t>0$?

Since the absolute values of $v(t)$ are increasing for $t>0$, we know that the slope of $h(t)$ will also be increasing, or getting steeper.

e. The values of $a(t)$ are always negative. What does this tell you about the slope of $v(t)$?

Since the values of $a(t)$ are always negative, we know that the slope of $v(t)$ is also negative, or sloping downwards.

f. The values of $a(t)$ are all the same. What does this tell you about the slope of $v(t)$?

Since the values of $a(t)$ are all the same, we know that the slope of $v(t)$ does not change, in other words, it is a straight line.

18. For the function

$$h(t) = -16t^2 + 30t + 5$$

where h is in feet and t is in seconds (as usual), and $h = 0$ is the ground, what is the object's initial speed (and direction)? What is the initial height?

For the function $h(t) = -16t^2 + 30t + 5$, the object's initial speed is 30 feet per second in the upward direction, and its initial height is 5 feet above the ground.

19. Answer the questions for the following graph:

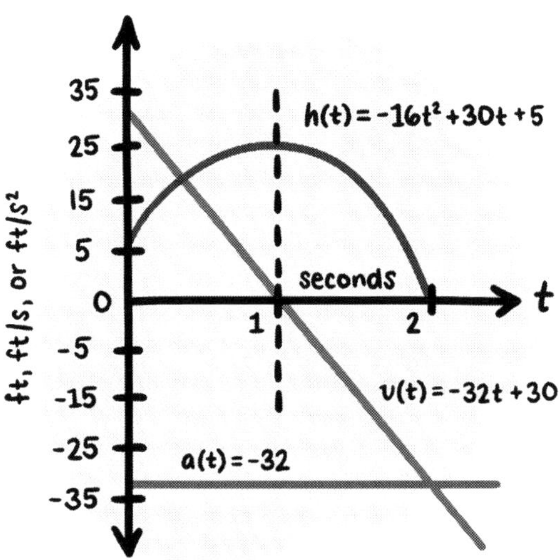

a. What is the slope of $h(t)$ at the dashed vertical line? What is the value of $v(t)$ at the dashed vertical line? What does this tell us about the motion of the object?

The slope of $h(t)$ at the dashed vertical line is 0. The value of $v(t)$ at the same time is also 0. Physically, this means that the object has come to a complete stop at this moment in time. It also means that the object has reached its maximum height since it will begin to travel downwards after this moment in time.

b. Find the time at which the object reaches its maximum height (and slowest speed).

In order to find the time at which the object reaches its maximum height, we need to remember that the object will reach that point when its velocity is equal to 0. Once we have our velocity function (the derivative of our height function) which is $v(t)$ = -32 +30, we can plug in our value for velocity (0) and solve for t. This gives us 0.9375 seconds, the time at which the object's velocity is zero and the object has reached its maximum height.

EXERCISE SOLUTIONS

1) $h(t) = -16t^2 + v_0 t + h_0$
   $v(t) = h'(t) = -32t + v_0$
   $a(t) = v'(t) = h''(t) = -32$

2) $h(t) = -16t^2 + v_0 t + h_0$

   $-16t^2 \rightarrow$ The effect (over time) that the force of gravity has on the height of the object. The negative sign indicates that the force is pulling downward.

   $v_0 t \rightarrow$ The effect (over time) that the initial velocity has on the height of the object.

   $h_0 \rightarrow$ The initial height of the object. That is, the effect (over time) that the initial height has on the height of the object, though this effect is constant.

3) a. $h(t) = -16t^2 + 16t \rightarrow$ An object thrown upward at a speed of 16 ft/s from an initial height of zero.

   b. $h(t) = -16t^2 + 16 \rightarrow$ An object dropped from a height of 16 ft.

   c. $h(t) = -16t^2 + 50t + 13 \rightarrow$ An object thrown *upward* at a speed of 50 ft/s from an initial height of 13 ft.

   d. $h(t) = -16t^2 - 50t + 13 \rightarrow$ An object thrown *downward* at a speed of 50 ft/s from an initial height of 13 ft.

4) a. $h(t) = -16t^2 + 70$
   b. $h(t) = -16t^2 + 70$
   c. $h(t) = -16t^2 + 15t + 10$
   d. $h(t) = -16t^2 - 100t + 1000$

5) All are cases of free fall and so all have the same acceleration due to gravity:

$$a = -32$$

6) a. We know that the slope of $h(t)$ is given by its derivative and that this derivative just is $v(t)$.
   So then, the value of $v(t)$ at $t = 0$ is $v(0) = 0$, since we know that the slope of $h(t) = 0$.
   These are the same thing.

b. The slope of $h(t)$ tells us two things here. First, after $t = 0$ the slope is negative and so we know that the direction the object is falling is downward. Second, the slope of $h(t)$ gets steeper as t increases. Since "steeper" means that the absolute value of the slope is increasing—and since $v(t)$ is the slope of $h(t)$— the speed is also increasing, that is, picking up speed as the object falls.

7) a. Since $v(t)$ is zero at $t = 0$, we know that the slope of $h(t)$ is also zero (i.e. flat).

b. Since $v(t)$ is negative for all values of $t \neq 0$, we know that $h(t)$ has a negative slope and therefore $h(t)$ slopes downward to the right.

c. The absolute value of $v(t)$ is increasing and so the slope of $h(t)$ is also increasing and therefore getting steeper.

d. The slope of $v(t)$ is constant and the values of $a(t)$ give the slope of $v(t)$, therefore the values of $a(t)$ are constant—a flat line. And so, of course, at $t = 0$ the slope is zero.

e. Remains constant (see d).

8) a. We know that for any case of free fall the acceleration "curve" is $a(t) = -32$. We also know that the value of $a(t)$ is the *slope* of $v(t)$. Since $a(t)$ crosses the vertical axis at –32, that is $a(0) = -32$, the slope of $v(t)$ at $t = 0$ is –32 or –32/1.

b. $a(t)$, which gives the slope of $v(t)$, is always negative and so $v(t)$ slopes downward to the right.

c. Since $a(t)$ is constant, so is the slope of $v(t)$.

9) a. To find the slope of $h(t)$ we can look at $v(t)$. The value of $v(t)$ at $t = 0$ is –30. That is, $v(0) = -30$. Therefore, the slope of $h(t)$ at $t = 0$ is –30 or –30/1.

b. The slope of $v(t)$ is the same everywhere (that is, it's constant) and is given by the values of $a(t)$, which is –32 or –32/1.

c. We know that the general from of $h(t)$ is

$$h(t) = -16t^2 + v_0 t + h_0 .$$

From the graph we see that $h_0 = 80$ ft and $v_0 = -30$ ft/s and so

$$h(t) = -16t^2 - 30t + 80 .$$

So then,

$$v(t) = h'(t) = -32t - 30$$

and

$$a(t) = h''(t) = v'(t) = -32 ,$$

as always.

CHAPTER 21 - THE ANTI-DERIVATIVE: UNDOING DERIVATIVES

ANSWERS TO THE STUDY QUESTIONS

1. What is calculus?

   Calculus is the mathematics of change.

2. What was the name of the shortcut rule that we used to find the derivative of power functions?

   The name of the shortcut rule that we used to find the derivative of power functions was the Power Rule.

3. What will we call the rule that allows us to find the original power function from its derivative? We came up with this rule in two stages. What are these two stages, very generally speaking?

   We will call the rule that allows us to find the original power function from its derivative the Reverse Power Rule. We will be coming up with this rule in two stages: first by finding an approximation and noting where this approximation falls short, and once we see its limitation, we'll move into stage two to overcome this limitation.

4. Where did we get the original Power Rule?

   We got the original Power Rule by using the Method of Increments.

5. Write out the first approximation of the Reverse Power Rule. What is the problem with our approximation?

   Our first approximation of the Reverse Power Rule is $Kx^n \rightarrow \frac{K}{n+1}x^{n+1}$. The problem with our approximation is that we may be missing some information. For example, if the original function was $g(x)=4x^3+8$, and its derivative is $12x^2$, then when we apply our Reverse Power Rule to $12x^2$, we end up with

$4x^3$ and not the original $4x^3+8$, so using our first approximation, we are off by the constant 8.

6. What is the correct version of the Reverse Power Rule?

   The correct version of the Reverse Power Rule is $Kx^n \rightarrow \frac{K}{n+1}x^{n+1} + C$.

7. What values can *C* stand for?

   ***C* can stand for any constant. It could be 2 or 10 or -10,036.12 or π or even simply 0.**

8. What is the notation for the anti-derivative of $f'(x)$?

   The notation for the anti-derivative of $f'(x)$ is $f(x)$.

9. What is the notation for the anti-derivative of $f(x)$?

   The notation for the anti-derivative of $f(x)$ is $F(x)$.

10. Why do we get into trouble if we try to use the Reverse Power Rule for $f(x)=1/x$?

    We get into trouble if we try to use the Reverse Power Rule for $f(x)=1/x$ because we will end up with a 0 in the denominator. Recall that $1/x$ can be written x^{-1}. Since our exponent is -1, our value for *n* using the Reverse Power Rule is also -1. Our Reverse Power Rule is $\frac{K}{n+1}x^{n+1} + C$, and substituting for *K* and *n* we get $\frac{1}{-1+1}x^{-1+1} + C$ which is $\frac{1}{0}x^0 + C$, but we've seen that dividing by 0 is meaningless.

11. What is the correct version of the Reverse Power Rule using our "capital letter" notation?

    The correct version of the Reverse Power Rule using our "capital letter" notation is $f(x) = Kx^n \rightarrow F(x)\frac{K}{n+1}x^{n+1} + C$.

12. What is the rule for finding the anti-derivative of the *sum* of power functions?

    The rule for finding the anti-derivative of the sum of power functions is, for $y(x)=f(x)+g(x)+u(x)$ ... the anti-derivative is $Y(x)=F(x)+G(x)+U(x)$ ...

13. What is the formula that tells us what we get when we take the derivative of the anti-derivative?

The formula that tells us what we get when we take the derivative of the anti-derivative is $\frac{d}{dx}\left[F(x)\right]=f(x)$.

14. To find $h(t)$ and $v(t)$ from $a(t)=-32$ in the case of free fall, why do we need "extra" information, that is, information in addition to $a(t)=-32$?

    To find $h(t)$ and $v(t)$ from $a(t)=-32$, we need extra information because we are taking the anti-derivative and will be left with a constant with an unknown value. We need extra information to determine the value of C.

15. One way to find $h(t)$ and $v(t)$ from $a(t)=-32$ is to take the anti-derivatives before finding the constants. In this case we arrive at

    $$h(t)=-16t\ \ +C_1t+C_2$$

    Why didn't we just use the same letter, C, for both of the constants?

    If we were to take the anti-derivative of $a(t)=-32$ twice without stopping to find the constants, we would end up with $h(t)=-16t^2+C_1t+C_2$. We don't write the same letter, C, for each of the constants because we don't know whether the second constant will be the same as the first—and in all likelihood it won't be the same, so we distinguish the two by writing C_1 and C_2.

16. What are the three main concepts in calculus and where do anti-derivatives fit into this list? What law holds these three concepts together?

    The three main concepts in calculus are the limit of a function, the derivative of a function, and the integral of a function. Anti-derivatives fit into this list with derivatives since they are closely related. The law that holds these three concepts together is called the fundamental theorem of calculus.

EXERCISE SOLUTIONS

1) a. $y'(x)=6x^3$

$$y(x)=\frac{6}{3+1}x^{3+1}+C=\frac{6}{4}x^4+C=\frac{3}{2}x^4+C$$

b. $g(x) = 5x^7 + 5x^5$

$$G(x) = \left[\frac{5}{7+1}x^{7+1} + C_1\right] + \left[\frac{5}{5+1}x^{5+1} + C_2\right] = \frac{5}{8}x^8 + \frac{5}{6}x^6 + C$$

c. $\frac{dy}{dx} = 2x^{100}$

$$y(x) = \frac{2}{100+1}x^{100+1} + C = \frac{2}{101}x^{101} + C$$

d. $z(x) = \frac{1}{x} = x^{\ 1}$ We can't use the Reverse Power Rule for $n = -1$.

e. $\frac{df}{dx} = \frac{8}{x^{-5}} + \frac{1}{x^{-1}} + \frac{55}{x^2} =$

$$= 8x^5 + x^1 + \frac{55}{x^2}$$

$$f(x) = \left[\frac{8}{5+1}x^{5+1} + C_1\right] + \left[\frac{1}{1+1}x^{1+1} + C_2\right] + \left[\frac{55}{-2+1}x^{-2+1} + C_3\right]$$

$$= \frac{8}{6}x^6 + \frac{1}{2}x^2 + \frac{55}{-1}x^{-1} + C =$$

$$= \frac{4}{3}x^6 + \frac{1}{2}x^2 - 55x^{-1} + C =$$

$$= \frac{4}{3}x^6 + \frac{1}{2}x^2 - \frac{55}{x} + C$$

f. $f(x) = \frac{17\sqrt{x}}{5} = \frac{17}{5}x^{\frac{1}{2}}$

$$F(x) = \frac{17}{5} \cdot \frac{1}{\frac{1}{2}+1}x^{\frac{1}{2}+1} + C = \frac{17}{5} \cdot \frac{1}{\frac{1}{2}+\frac{2}{2}}x^{\frac{1}{2}+\frac{2}{2}} + C =$$

$$= \frac{17}{5} \cdot \frac{1}{\frac{3}{2}}x^{\frac{3}{2}} + C = \frac{17}{5} \cdot \frac{2}{3}x^{\frac{3}{2}} + C =$$

$$= \frac{34}{15}x^{\frac{3}{2}} + C$$

g. $y'(z) = \sqrt[4]{z^3} = z^{\frac{3}{4}}$

$$y(z) = \frac{1}{\frac{3}{4}+\frac{4}{4}}z^{\frac{3}{4}+\frac{4}{4}} + C = \frac{4}{7}z^{\frac{7}{4}} + C$$

h. $f(x)=9x^7-\pi\sqrt[3]{x}+\dfrac{1}{\sqrt{x}}+x=9x^7-\pi x^{\frac{1}{3}}+x^{-\frac{1}{2}}+x$

$$F(x)=\left[\frac{9}{7+1}x^{7+1}+C_1\right]-\left[\frac{\pi}{\frac{1}{3}+\frac{3}{3}}x^{\frac{1}{3}+\frac{3}{3}}+C_2\right]+\left[\frac{1}{-\frac{1}{2}+\frac{2}{2}}x^{-\frac{1}{2}+\frac{2}{2}}+C_3\right]+$$

$$+\left[\frac{1}{1+1}x^{1+1}+C_4\right]=$$

NOTE: The negative sign in front of the second parentheses gets distributed, but a constant minus a constant is still a constant.

$$=\frac{9}{8}x^8-\frac{\pi}{\frac{4}{3}}x^{\frac{4}{3}}+\frac{1}{\frac{3}{2}}x^{\frac{3}{2}}+\frac{1}{\frac{1}{2}}x^{\frac{1}{2}}+C=$$

$$F(x)=\frac{9}{8}x^8-\frac{3\pi}{4}x^{\frac{4}{3}}+\frac{2}{3}x^{\frac{3}{2}}+2\sqrt{x}+C$$

i. $y(x)=7x^{\pi}$

$$Y(x)=\frac{7}{\pi+1}x^{\pi+1}+C$$

j. $g'(x)=-6x^{-6}+2x^{-\frac{2}{5}}+\dfrac{1}{x^{-\frac{1}{2}}}=-6x^{-6}+2x^{-\frac{2}{5}}+x^{\frac{1}{2}}$

$$g(x)=\left[\frac{-6}{-6+1}x^{-6+1}+C_1\right]+\left[\frac{2}{-\frac{2}{5}+\frac{5}{5}}x^{-\frac{2}{5}+\frac{5}{5}}+C_2\right]+\left[\frac{1}{\frac{1}{2}+\frac{2}{2}}x^{\frac{1}{2}+\frac{2}{2}}+C_3\right]=$$

$$=\frac{6}{5}x^{-5}+\frac{2}{\frac{3}{5}}x^{\frac{3}{5}}+\frac{1}{\frac{3}{2}}x^{\frac{3}{2}}+C=$$

$$=\frac{6}{5}x^{-5}+\frac{10}{3}x^{\frac{3}{5}}+\frac{2}{3}x^{\frac{3}{2}}+C=$$

$$g(x)=\frac{6}{5x^5}+\frac{10}{3}\sqrt[5]{x^3}+\frac{2}{3}\sqrt{x^3}+C$$

k. $f'(x)=ax^n$

$$f(x)=\frac{a}{n+1}x^{n+1}+C$$

2) $f(x)=\frac{a}{n+1}x^{n+1}+C \quad =\frac{a}{n+1}x^{n+1}+Cx^{0}$

$f'(x)=(n+1)\frac{a}{(n+1)}x^{(n+1)-1}+0\cdot C\,x^{0-1}=$

$f'(x)=a\,x^{n}$

3) a. We begin with $a(t)=-32$ for any freefall case. To find $v(t)$ we note that $v(0)=0$ because the object was dropped.

$$v(t)=A(t)=\frac{-32}{0+1}t^{0+1}+C=-32t+C$$
$$v_0=v(0)=0=-32(0)+C \quad \Rightarrow \quad C=0$$

Therefore,

$$v(t)=-32t$$

Now, we know that $h(0)=100$, and so

$$h(t)=v(t)=\frac{-32}{1+1}t^{1+1}+C=\frac{-32}{2}t^{2}+C=-16t^{2}+C$$
$$h(0)=100=-16(0)^{2}+C \quad \Rightarrow \quad C=100$$

Therefore,

$$h(t)=-16t^{2}+100$$

b. $a(t)=-32$, which is the same for all free fall cases.

$$v(t)=\frac{-32}{0+1}t^{0+1}+C=-32t+C$$
$$v(0)=25=-32(0)+C \quad \Rightarrow \quad C=25$$

Therefore,

$$v(t)=-32t+25$$

$$h(t)=V(t)=\frac{-32}{1+1}t^{1+1}+C_1+\frac{25t}{0+1}t^{0+1}+C_2=-16t^{2}+25t+C$$
$$h(0)=50=-16(0)^{2}+25(0)+C \quad \Rightarrow \quad C=50$$

Therefore,

$$h(t)=-16t^{2}+25t+50$$

c. As usual $a(t)=-32$

$$v(t)=A(t)=\frac{-32}{0+1}t^{0+1}+C_1=-32t+C_1$$

From the graph we see that at $t=0$, $v(t)=0$ and so

$$v(0)=0=-32(0)+C_1 \quad \Rightarrow \quad C_1=0$$

Therefore,

$$v(t)=-32t$$

$$h(t)=\frac{-32}{1+1}t^{1+1}+C_2=-16t^2+C_2$$

From the graph we see that at $t=0$, $h(t)=80$ and so

$$h(0)=80=-16(0)^2+C_2 \quad \Rightarrow \quad C_2=80$$

Therefore,

$$h(t)=-16t^2+80$$

d. $a(t)=-32$

$$v(t)=A(t)=\frac{-32}{0+1}t^{0+1}+C_1=-32t+C_1$$

From the graph we see that at $t=0$, $v(t)=30$ and so

$$v(0)=30=-32(0)+C_1 \quad \Rightarrow \quad C_1=30$$

Therefore,

$$v(t)=-32t+30$$

$$\begin{aligned} h(t)=V(t)&=\frac{-32}{1+1}t^{1+1}C_2+\frac{30}{0+1}t^{0+1}+C_3 \\ &=-16t^2+30t+C \end{aligned}$$

From the graph we see that at $t=0$, $h(t)=5$ and so

$$h(0)=5=-16(0)^2+30(0)+C \quad \Rightarrow \quad C=5$$

Therefore,

$$h(t)=-16t^2+30t+5$$

CHAPTER 22 - DEFINING THE INTEGRAL

ANSWERS TO THE STUDY QUESTIONS

1. What is the method of exhaustion?

   The method of exhaustion is a method of finding the area of a shape with curved borders by inscribing or circumscribing simpler shapes. We can estimate the area of a complicated shape by dividing the shape into mini-areas whose areas are easy to calculate and adding up these mini-areas.

2. From the figures in the text, draw what the method of exhaustion might look like for approximating the area of a circle for both underestimating and overestimating the area.

   See figures 22.1b and 22.1c.

3. What do we call the case of overestimating? Of underestimating?

   In the case of overestimating, we say "circumscribed," and in the case of underestimating, we say "inscribed."

4. What does "exhaustion" mean in the context of the method of exhaustion?

   In the context of the method of exhaustion, "exhaustion" means "roughly."

5. What happens to the approximation of the area as the number of mini-areas increases?

   As the number of mini-areas increases, the approximation of the area gets closer to the shape's actual area.

6. What letter did we use to represent the number of mini-areas?

   We used the letter to represent the number of mini-areas.

7. In the text we gave three characteristics of the integral. Write them out.

The first characteristic of the integral is that an integral is an area. The second is that an integral is a sum of mini-areas. The third is that, for an integral, the number of mini-areas approaches infinity.

8. What concept or tool of calculus—a concept that is related to the word "approach"—was added to the method of exhaustion to get the notion of an integral?

   The concept or tool of calculus which is related to the word "approach" and which was added to the method of exhaustion is the limit.

9. Why is it odd to say that "n approaches ∞"?

   It is odd to say that n approaches ∞ because, no matter how high you count, you're never any closer to infinity than when you began.

10. In words, what is S_n?

    In words, S_n is the summation of n mini-areas.

11. In S_n and the limit notation, what is the formula for the total area?

    In S_n and limit notation, the formula for the total area is $A = \lim_{n \to \infty} S_n$.

12. In formula form, what is the definition of an integral?

    In formula form, the definition of an integral is $A = \lim_{n \to \infty} S_n$.

13. What happens to the size of the mini-areas as n approaches ∞?

    As n approaches ∞, the size of the mini-areas approach 0.

14. Why do Cartesian coordinates help us when calculating the area of shapes?

    Cartesian coordinates help us when calculating the area of shapes because we can graph shapes in Cartesian coordinates.

15. For the function $y(x)=x^2$, sketch the drawing that shows the area under the curve in Figure 22.3a.

    See figure 22.3a.

16. What letters did we use to represent the two endpoints (where the sides run into the x-axis) of the area?

We used the letters *a* and *b* to represent the two endpoints of the area.

17. What is the area formula for a rectangle?

    The formula for the area of a rectangle is $A = bh$, that is, base times height.

18. Draw the graph in Figure 22.3c. (Eventually make sure you can draw it from memory.) Are the rectangles inscribed or circumscribed?

    See figure 22.3c. The rectangles are inscribed (underestimated).

19. Draw the graph in Figure 22.3d. What is important to notice about the gaps?

    See figure 22.3d. It is important to notice that the gaps in figure 22.3d are large which means that our approximation of the area won't be especially close to the actual area under the curve.

20. As we go from Figure 22.3d, to Figure 22.3e, to Figure 22.3f, what happens to the gaps? What happens to the mini-areas?

    As we go from figure 22.3d to figure 22.3e and figure 22.3f, the gaps get smaller and smaller. As we move from figure to figure, the mini-areas get smaller and smaller.

21. Draw the graph in Figure 22.3g. Make it large enough to draw the details.

    See figure 22.3g.

22. In Figure 22.3g, what is important about where the rectangles touch the curve of $y(x)=x^2$? What symbol are we using to refer to the width (i.e., base) of each mini-rectangle? What symbol for the height? How would we calculate that height?

    In figure 22.3g, the important thing about where the rectangle touches the curve of $y(x)=x^2$ is that the rectangle touches the curve at a single point. We are using the symbol Δx to refer to the width (i.e., base) of each mini-rectangle. The mini-rectangles height is the value of $y(x)$ at the rectangle's point of contact with $y(x)$. We can calculate the value by plugging the appropriate -value into $y(x)=x^2$.

23. Draw Figure 22.3h. What are the coordinates of the point where the rectangle touches the curve $y(x)=x^2$? What is the formula for the height of the rectangle? Where did we get that formula?

    See figure 22.3h. In figure 22.3h, the coordinates of the point where the rectangle touches the curve $y(x)=x^2$ are (x_1, y_1). The formula for the height of the rectangle in figure 22.3h is $y_1=(x_1)^2$. We got that formula from the original function $y(x)=x^2$.

24. Looking at mini-area 1 in Figure 22.3i, what is the formula for its area?

    The formula for the area of mini-area 1 in figure 22.3i is $A_1=y_1\cdot\Delta x$.

25. In terms of A_i's what is the formula for S_n?

    In terms of A_i's, the formula for S_n is $S_n = A_1 + A_2 + A_3 + A_4 + \cdots + A_n$.

26. In terms of y_i's and Δx's, what is the formula for S_n?

    In terms of y_i's and Δx's, the formula for S_n is $S_n = (y_1\cdot\Delta x) + (y_2\cdot\Delta x) + (y_3\cdot\Delta x) + (y_4\cdot\Delta x) + \cdots + (y_n\cdot\Delta x)$.

27. In terms of S_n and the limit notation, give the definition of the integral.

    In terms of S_n and the limit notation, the definition of the integral is $A = \lim\limits_{n\to\infty} S_n$.

28. In terms of A_i's and the limit notation, give the definition of the integral.

    In terms of A_i's and the limit notation, the definition of the integral is $A = \lim\limits_{n\to\infty}\left[A_1 + A_2 + A_3 + A_4 + \cdots + A_n\right]$.

29. In terms of y's and Δx's and the limit notation, give the definition of the integral.

    In terms of 's and 's and the limit notation, the definition of the integral is $A = \lim\limits_{n\to\infty}\left[(y_1 \cdot \Delta x) + (y_2 \cdot \Delta x) + (y_3 \cdot \Delta x) + (y_4 \cdot \Delta x) + \cdots + (y_n \cdot \Delta x)\right]$.

30. Draw Figure 22.4a, the circumscribed case. What important details change from the inscribed case? Are any of the formulas or symbols different?

    See figure 22.4a. A few important details change from the inscribed case to the circumscribed case. In the circumscribed case, the mini-rectangles now rise above the function's curve and the rectangles touch the function's curve at the top-right corner of the rectangle, whereas the inscribed mini-rectangles

were below the curve and touched at the top-left corner of the rectangle. None of the formulas or symbols are different in either case.

31. Is the definition of the integral any different if we begin with the circumscribed case?

    The definition of the integral is no different when we begin with the circumscribed case instead of the inscribed case.

32. What will we do in the following chapter? What method will we use to do this?

    In the following chapter, we will calculate the areas of complicated shapes. To do this, we will use the Method of Summation.

CHAPTER 23 - USING THE METHOD OF SUMMATION TO CALCULATE INTEGRALS

ANSWERS TO THE STUDY QUESTIONS

1. In words, what is an integral?

   An integral is an area: the sum of mini-areas as n approaches ∞.

2. In symbols, what is an integral?

   In symbols, an integral is $A = \lim_{n \to \infty} S_n$.

3. What was the long method of taking the derivative of a function? How did we take a shortcut?

   The long method of taking the derivative of a function was the Method of Increments. We took a shortcut by using the Power Rule.

4. What is the name of the long method for taking the integral of a function?

   The name of the long method for taking the integral of a function is the Method of Summation.

5. What are the two main steps of the Method of Summation? Which is the hardest step?

   The two main steps of the Method of Summation are, first, to find a formula for S_n in terms of n, and second, to take the limit of S_n as $n \longrightarrow \infty$. The first step is the hardest.

6. What is an ellipsis? How will the special summation rules help us with it?

   An ellipsis tells us to continue with the pattern. The special summation rules will help us to get rid of the ellipsis.

7. In terms of y's and Δx's, what is the formula for S_n?

   In terms of y_i's and Δx's, the formula for S_n is $S_n = (y_1 \cdot \Delta x) + (y_2 \cdot \Delta x) + (y_3 \cdot \Delta x) + (y_4 \cdot \Delta x) + \cdots + (y_n \cdot \Delta x)$.

8. What does the bar under S_n indicate about S_n?

   The bar under S_n indicates that S_n is an underestimation for finite *n*'s.

9. In the symbols y_i and x_i, what does the i stand for?

   In the symbols y_i and x_i, the i stands for each rectangle's identifying number.

10. What does the bar over S_n indicate about S_n?

    The bar over S_n indicates that S_n is an overestimation for finite *n*'s.

11. For Example 1 the summation of *n* mini-areas was given by

$$\underline{S_n} = 16 - \frac{8}{n}$$

while for Example 2 the summation of *n* mini-areas was given by

$$\overline{S_n} = 16 + \frac{8}{n}$$

What do the positive and negative signs tell us?

The negative sign from the summation of *n* mini-areas in example 1 came from the fact that the mini-rectangles were inscribed. The positive sign from the summation of *n* mini-areas in example 2 came from the fat that the mini-rectangles were circumscribed.

12. What is

$$\lim_{n \to \infty} S_n$$

in terms of our elongated "s" integral notation? What does "*ydx*" as a whole stand for? What does *y* stand for? What does *dx* stand for?

In terms of our elongated "s" integral notation, $\lim_{x \to \infty} S_n$ *is* $\int_a^b ydx$. As a whole, "*ydx*" stands for the area of each infinitely thin mini-rectangle. *y* stands for the height of each mini-rectangle, and *dx* stands for the base of each mini-rectangle.

13. In terms of the limit notation what is *dx*?

    In terms of the limit notation, *dx* stands for $\lim_{\Delta x \to 0} \Delta x$.

14. What do the *a* and *b* stand for in the formula

$$\int_a^b y dx$$

In the formula $\int_a^b y dx$, the a and b stand for the x-values of the endpoints of the entire area's base.

15. What does "$f(x)dx$" as a whole stand for in the formula

$$\int_a^b f(x) dx$$

What does $f(x)$ stand for? What does dx stand for?

As a whole, "$f(x)dx$" stands for the area of each infinitely thin mini-rectangle. $f(x)$ stands for the height of each mini-rectangle, and dx stands for the base of each mini-rectangle.

16. What are the three central concepts in calculus? What is the "core" of calculus?

The three central concepts in calculus are the limit, derivative, and integral of a function. The core of calculus is the Fundamental Theorem of Calculus.

EXERCISE SOLUTIONS

1) See Example 1 in chapter.
2) See Example 2 in chapter.
3) See Example 3 in chapter.
4) See Example 4 in chapter.
5) Area, A, below $y=x^2$ between $x=0$ and $x=2$:

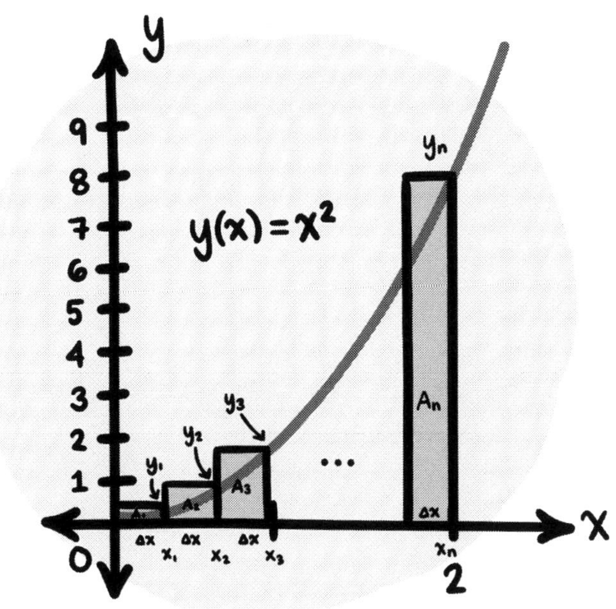

i	x_i	y_i
1	$x_1 = \Delta x$	$y_1 = (\Delta x)^2 = (\Delta x)^2$
2	$x_2 = 2\Delta x$	$y_2 = (2\Delta x)^2 = 4(\Delta x)^2$
3	$x_3 = 3\Delta x$	$y_3 = (3\Delta x)^2 = 9(\Delta x)^2$
$\vdots$	$\vdots$	$\vdots$
n	$x_n = n\Delta x$	$y_{\mathrm{n}} = (n\Delta x)^2 = n^2(\Delta x)^2$

$$\Delta x = \frac{2-0}{n} = \frac{2}{n}$$

$$\begin{aligned}
\overline{S}_n &= (\Delta x)^2\Delta x + 4(\Delta x)^2\Delta x + 9(\Delta x)^2\Delta x + \cdots + n^2(\Delta x)^2\Delta x = \\
&= (\Delta x)^3 + 4(\Delta x)^3 + 9(\Delta x)^3 + \cdots + n^2(\Delta x)^3 = \\
&= (\Delta x)^3[1^2 + 2^2 + 3^2 + \cdots + n^2] = (\Delta x)^3\left[\frac{n^3}{3} + \frac{n^2}{2} + \frac{n}{6}\right] = \left[\frac{2}{n}\right]^3\left[\frac{n^3}{3} + \frac{n^2}{2} + \frac{n}{6}\right] \\
&= \frac{8}{n_3}\left[\frac{n^3}{3} + \frac{n^2}{2} + \frac{n}{6}\right] = \frac{8}{3} + \frac{4}{n} + \frac{4}{3n^2} \quad \Rightarrow
\end{aligned}$$

$$\Rightarrow \quad A = \int_0^2 x^2 dx = \lim_{n\to\infty}\left[\frac{8}{3} + \frac{4}{n} + \frac{4}{3n^2}\right] = \frac{8}{3}$$

6) Integral of $y=3x$ from $x=1$ to $x=5$:

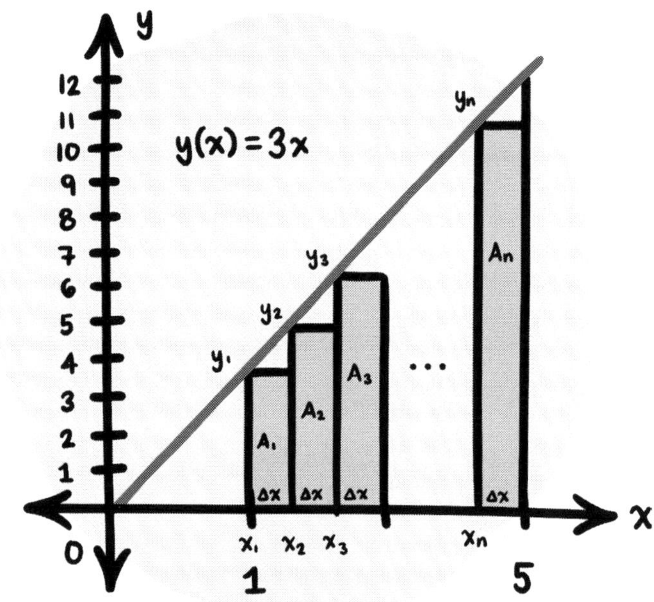

i	x_i	y_i
1	$x_1=1$	$y_1=3(1)=3$
2	$x_2=1+\Delta x$	$y_2=3(1+\Delta x)$
3	$x_3=1+2\Delta x$	$y_3=3(1+2\Delta x)$
$\vdots$	$\vdots$	$\vdots$
n	$x_n=1+(n-1)\Delta x$	$y_n=3(1+(n-1)\Delta x)$

$$\underline{S}_n = y_1\Delta x + y_2\Delta x + y_3\Delta x + \cdots + y_n\Delta x =$$
$$=3\Delta x + 3(1+\Delta x)\Delta x + 3(1+2\Delta x)\Delta x + \cdots + 3(1+(n-1)\Delta x)\Delta x =$$
$$= 3\Delta x + 3\Delta x + 3(\Delta x)^2 + 3\Delta x + 6(\Delta x)^2 + \cdots + 3\Delta x + 3(n-1)(\Delta x)^2 =$$
$$= 3n\Delta x + 3(\Delta x)^2 + 6(\Delta x)^2 + \cdots + 3(n-1)(\Delta x)^2 =$$
$$= 3n\Delta x + 3(\Delta x)^2 \underbrace{\left[1+2+\cdots+(n-1)\right]}_{\frac{n(n-1)}{2}} =$$

Remember, n is the number of rectangles

$$= 3n\Delta x + 3(\Delta x)^2\left[\frac{n(n-1)}{2}\right] =$$

We need Δx in terms of n:

$$\Delta x = \frac{5-1}{n} = \frac{4}{n}$$

$$= \cancel{3n}\left(\frac{4}{\cancel{n}}\right) + 3\left(\frac{4}{n}\right)^2\left[\frac{n(n-1)}{2}\right] = 12 + 3\cdot\frac{16}{n^2}\left[\frac{n(n-1)}{2}\right] =$$

$$= 12 + \frac{24(n-1)}{n} = 12 + 24\left[\frac{n}{n} - \frac{1}{n}\right] = 12 + 24\left[1 - \frac{1}{n}\right] =$$

$$= 12 + 24 - \frac{24}{n} = 36 - \frac{24}{n}$$

$$\Rightarrow \quad A = \int_1^5 3x\,dx = \lim_{n\to\infty} \underline{S}_n = \lim_{n\to\infty}\left[36 - \frac{24}{n}\right] = 36$$

7) Integral of y=3x from x=1 to x=5:

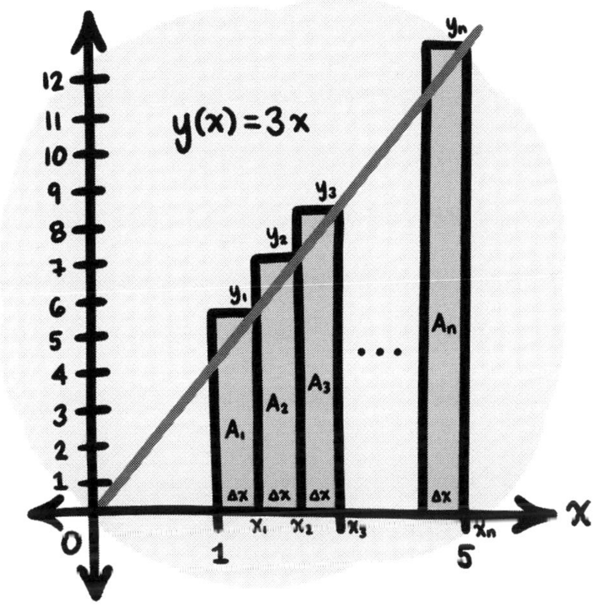

i	x_i	y_i
1	$x_1 = 1 + \Delta x$	$y_1 = 3(1 + \Delta x)$
2	$x_2 = 1 + 2\Delta x$	$y_2 = 3(1 + 2\Delta x)$
3	$x_3 = 1 + 3\Delta x$	$y_3 = 3(1 + 3\Delta x)$
$\vdots$	$\vdots$	$\vdots$
n	$x_n = 1 + n\Delta x$	$y_n = 3(1 + n\Delta x)$

$$\underset{\rightarrow n}{S} = y_1\Delta x + y_2\Delta x + y_3\Delta x + \cdots + y_n\Delta x =$$
$$= 3(1+\Delta x)\Delta x + 3(1+2\Delta x)\Delta x + 3(1+3\Delta x)\Delta x + \cdots + 3(1+n\Delta x)\Delta x =$$
$$= 3\Delta x + 3(\Delta x)^2 + 3\Delta x + 6(\Delta x)^2 + 3\Delta x + 9(\Delta x)^2 + \cdots + 3\Delta x + 3n(\Delta x)^2 =$$
$$= 3n\Delta x + 3(\Delta x)^2 + 6(\Delta x)^2 + 69\Delta x)^2 + \cdots + 3n(\Delta x)^2 =$$
$$= 3n\Delta x + 3(\Delta x)^2 \underbrace{\left[1+2+\cdots+n\right]}_{\frac{n(n-1)}{2}} =$$
$$= 3n\Delta x + 3(\Delta x)^2 \left[\frac{n(n+1)}{2}\right]$$

We need Δx in terms of n:

$$\Delta x = \frac{5-1}{n} = \frac{4}{n}$$

$$\underset{\rightarrow n}{S} = 3n\left(\frac{4}{n}\right) + 3\left(\frac{4}{n}\right)^2 \left[\frac{n(n+1)}{2}\right] = 12 + 3\cdot\frac{16}{n^2}\left[\frac{n(n+1)}{2}\right] =$$
$$= 12 + \frac{24(n+1)}{n} = 12 + 24 + \frac{24}{n} = 36 + \frac{24}{n}$$

$$\Rightarrow \quad A = \int_1^5 3x\,dx = \lim_{n\to\infty} \underset{\rightarrow n}{S} = \lim_{n\to\infty}\left[36 + \frac{24}{n}\right] = 36$$

8) Integral of $y=x^2$ from $x=0$ to $x=5$:

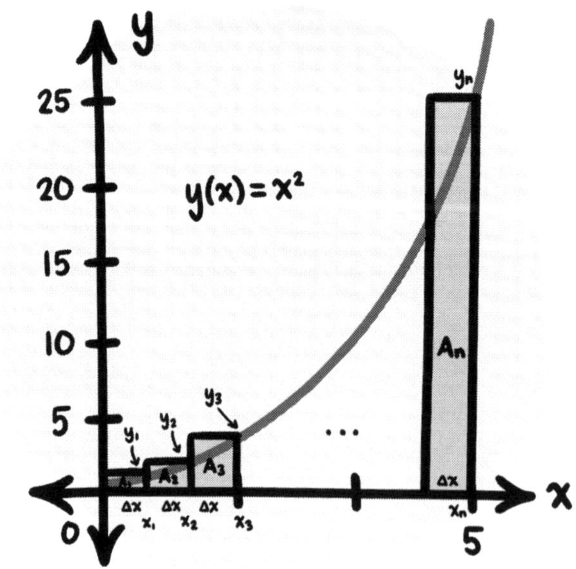

i	x_i	y_i
1	$x_1 = \Delta x$	$y_1 = (\Delta x)^2$
2	$x_2 = 2\Delta x$	$y_2 = (2\Delta x)^2 = 4(\Delta x)^2$
3	$x_3 = 3\Delta x$	$y_3 = (3\Delta x)^2 = 9(\Delta x)^2$
$\vdots$	$\vdots$	$\vdots$
n	$x_n = n\Delta x$	$y_n = (n\Delta x)^2 = n^2(\Delta x)^2$

$$\overline{S}_n = (\Delta x)^2 \Delta x + 4(\Delta x)^2 \Delta x + 9(\Delta x)^2 \Delta x + \cdots + n^2(\Delta x)^2 \Delta x =$$

$$= (\Delta x)^3 + 4(\Delta x)^3 + 9(\Delta x)^3 + \cdots + n^2(\Delta x)^3 =$$

$$= (\Delta x)^3 \underbrace{\left[1^2 + 2^2 + 3^2 + \cdots + n^2\right]}_{\frac{n^3}{3}+\frac{n^2}{2}+\frac{n}{6}} =$$

$$= (\Delta x)^3 \left[\frac{n^3}{3} + \frac{n^2}{2} + \frac{n}{6}\right]$$

We need Δx in terms of n:

$$\Delta x = \frac{5-0}{n} = \frac{5}{n}$$

$$\underline{S}_n = \left[\frac{5}{n}\right]^3 \left[\frac{n^3}{3} + \frac{n^2}{2} + \frac{n}{6}\right] = \frac{125}{n^3}\left[\frac{n^3}{3} + \frac{n^2}{2} + \frac{n}{6}\right] =$$

$$= 125\left[\frac{1}{3} + \frac{1}{2n} + \frac{1}{6n^2}\right] = \frac{125}{3} + \frac{125}{2n} + \frac{125}{6n^2}$$

$$\Rightarrow \qquad A = \int_0^5 x^2 dx = \lim_{n\to\infty}\left[\frac{125}{3} + \frac{125}{2n} + \frac{125}{6n^2}\right] = \frac{125}{3}$$

9) Integral of $y=x^2$ from $x=1$ to $x=5$:

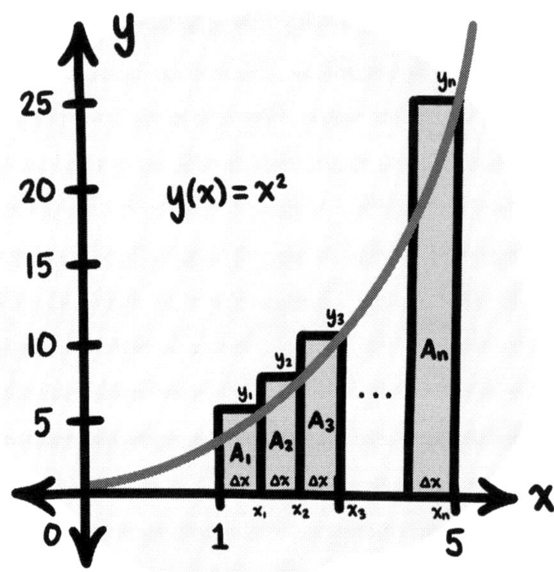

i	x_i	y_i
1	$x_1 = 1 + \Delta x$	$y_1 = (1 + \Delta x)^2$
2	$x_2 = 1 + 2\Delta x$	$y_2 = (1 + 2\Delta x)^2$
3	$x_3 = 1 + 3\Delta x$	$y_3 = (1 + 3\Delta x)^2$
$\vdots$	$\vdots$	$\vdots$
n	$x_n = 1 + n\Delta x$	$y_n = (1 + n\Delta x)^2$

$$\begin{aligned}
\overline{S}_n &= \Delta x(1+\Delta x)^2 + \Delta x(1+2\Delta x)^2 + \Delta x(1+3\Delta x)^2 + \cdots + \Delta x(1+n\Delta x)^2 = \\
&= \Delta x(1+\Delta x)(1+\Delta x) + \Delta x(1+2\Delta x)(1+2\Delta x) + \cdots + \Delta x(1+n\Delta x)^2 = \\
&= \Delta x[1+2\Delta x+(\Delta x)^2] + \Delta x[1+4\Delta x+2^2(\Delta x)^2] + \cdots + \Delta x[1+2n\Delta x+n^2(\Delta x)^2] = \\
&= \Delta x + 2(\Delta x)^2(\Delta x)^3 + \Delta x + 4(\Delta x)^2 + 2^2(\Delta x)^3 + \cdots + \Delta x + 2n(\Delta x)^2 + n^2(\Delta x)^3 = \\
&= n\Delta x + \left[2(\Delta x)^2 + 4(\Delta x)^2 + \cdots + 2n(\Delta x)^2\right] + \left[(\Delta x)^3 + 2^2(\Delta x)^3 + \cdots + n^2(\Delta x)^3\right] = \\
&= n\Delta x + 2(\Delta x)^2 \underbrace{[1+2+\cdots+n]}_{\frac{n}{2}(1+n)} + (\Delta x)^3 \underbrace{[1^2+2^2+\cdots+n^2]}_{\frac{n^3}{3}+\frac{n^2}{2}+\frac{n}{6}} = \\
&= n\Delta x + 2(\Delta x)^2\left[\frac{n}{2}(1+n)\right] + (\Delta x)^3\left[\frac{n^3}{3}+\frac{n^2}{2}+\frac{n}{6}\right] \quad \Rightarrow
\end{aligned}$$

$$\Delta x = \frac{5-1}{n} = \frac{4}{n}$$

$$\overline{S}_n = n\left(\frac{4}{n}\right)+2\left(\frac{4}{n}\right)^2\left[\frac{n}{2}(1+n)\right]+\left(\frac{4}{n}\right)^3\left[\frac{n^3}{3}+\frac{n^2}{2}+\frac{n}{6}\right]$$
$$= 4+\frac{32}{n^2}\left[\frac{n}{2}(1+n)\right]+\frac{64}{n^3}\left[\frac{n^3}{3}+\frac{n^2}{2}+\frac{n}{6}\right]$$
$$= 4+\frac{16}{n}(1+n)+\frac{64}{3}+\frac{32}{n}+\frac{64}{6n^2}$$
$$= 4+\frac{16}{n}+16+\frac{64}{3}+\frac{32}{n}+\frac{32}{3n^2} = \frac{12+48+64}{3}+\frac{48}{n}+\frac{32}{3n^2}$$
$$= \frac{124}{3}+\frac{48}{n}+\frac{32}{3n^2}$$
$$A = \int_1^5 x^2 dx = \lim_{n\to\infty} \overline{S}_n = \lim_{n\to\infty}\left[\frac{124}{3}+\frac{48}{n}+\frac{32}{3n^2}\right] = \frac{124}{3}$$

10) Area, A, below $y=x^2$ between $x=1$ and $x=5$:

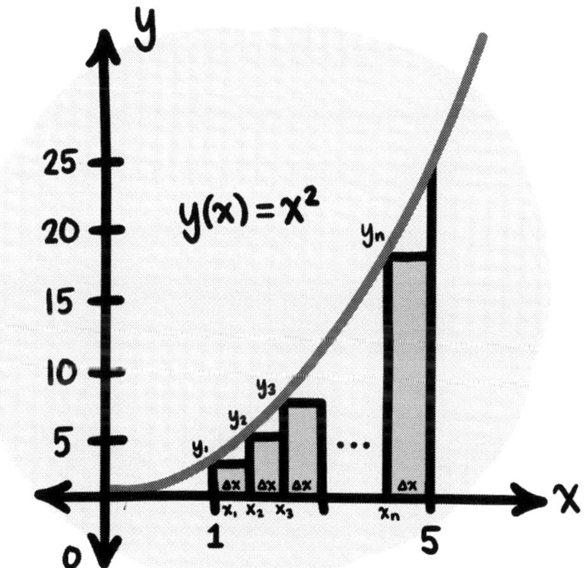

i	x_i	y_i
1	$x_1 = 1$	$y_1 = (1)^2 = 1$
2	$x_2 = 1+\Delta x$	$y_2 = (1+\Delta x)^2$
3	$x_3 = 1+2\Delta x$	$y_3 = (1+2\Delta x)^2$
$\vdots$	$\vdots$	$\vdots$
n	$x_n = 1+(n-1)\Delta x$	$y_n = (1+(n-1)\Delta x)^2$

$$\underline{S}_n = \Delta x \cdot 1 + \Delta x(1+\Delta x)^2 + \Delta x(1+2\Delta x)^2 + \cdots + \Delta x(1+(n-1)\Delta x)^2 =$$
$$= \Delta x + \Delta x(1+\Delta x)(1+\Delta x) + \Delta x(1+2\Delta x)(1+2\Delta x) + \cdots +$$
$$+\Delta x(1+(n-1)\Delta x)(1+(n-1)\Delta x) =$$
$$= \Delta x + \Delta x(1+2\Delta x(\Delta x)^2) + \Delta x(1+4\Delta x + 2^2(\Delta x)^2) + \cdots +$$
$$+\Delta x(1+2(n-1)\Delta x + (n-1)^2(\Delta x)^2) =$$
$$= \Delta x + \Delta x + 2(\Delta x)^2 + (\Delta x)^3 + \Delta x + 4(\Delta x)^2 + 2^2(\Delta x)^3 + \cdots +$$
$$+\Delta x + 2(\Delta x)^2(n-1) + (n-1)^2(\Delta x)^3 =$$

$$= n\Delta x + \left[2(\Delta x)^2 + 4(\Delta x)^2 + \cdots + 2(n-1)(\Delta x)^2\right] + \cdots +$$
$$+\left[(\Delta x)^3 + 2^2(\Delta x)^3 + (n-1)^2(\Delta x)^3\right] =$$
$$= n\Delta x + 2(\Delta x)^2 \underbrace{[1+2+\cdots+(n-1)]}_{\frac{n(n-1)}{2}} + (\Delta x)^3 \underbrace{[1^2+2^2+\cdots+(n-1)^2]}_{\frac{n^3}{3}-\frac{n^2}{2}+\frac{n}{6}} =$$
$$= n\Delta x + 2(\Delta x)^2\left[\frac{n(n-1)}{2}\right] + (\Delta x)^3\left[\frac{n^3}{3}-\frac{n^2}{2}+\frac{n}{6}\right] \quad \Rightarrow$$
$$\Delta x = \frac{5-1}{n} = \frac{4}{n}$$
$$\underline{S}_n = n\left[\frac{4}{n}\right] + 2\left[\frac{4}{n}\right]^2\left[\frac{n(n-1)}{2}\right] + \left[\frac{4}{n}\right]^3\left[\frac{n^3}{3}-\frac{n^2}{2}+\frac{n}{6}\right] =$$
$$= 4 + \frac{2\cdot 16}{n^2}\left[\frac{n(n-1)}{2}\right]^2 + \frac{64}{n^3}\left[\frac{n^3}{3}-\frac{n^2}{2}+\frac{n}{6}\right] =$$
$$= 4 + \frac{16}{n}(n-1) + \frac{64}{3} - \frac{64}{2n} + \frac{64}{6n^2} = 4 + 16 - \frac{16}{n} + \frac{64}{3} - \frac{32}{n} + \frac{32}{3n^2} =$$
$$= \frac{12+48+64}{3} - \frac{48}{n} + \frac{32}{3n^2} = \frac{124}{3} - \frac{48}{n} + \frac{32}{3n^2} \quad \Rightarrow$$

$$A = \int_1^5 x^2 dx = \lim_{n\to\infty}\left[\frac{124}{3} - \frac{48}{n} + \frac{32}{3n^2}\right] = \frac{124}{3}$$

CHAPTER 24 - THE FUNDAMENTAL THEOREM OF CALCULUS

ANSWERS TO THE STUDY QUESTIONS

1. What are the three central concepts in calculus? What ties them all together?

   The three central concepts in calculus are the limit, derivative, and integral of a function. The Fundamental Theorem of Calculus ties them all together.

2. In terms of limits, what is formula for the definition of a derivative?

   The formula for the definition of a derivative is $\frac{dy}{dx} = \lim_{\Delta x \to 0}\left(\frac{\Delta y}{\Delta x}\right)$.

3. What is the geometrical interpretation of the derivative?

   Geometrically, the derivative of a function is a function's slope.

4. In terms of limits, what is formula for the definition of an integral?

   The formula for the definition of an integral is $\int_a^b y(x)dx = \lim_{n \to \infty} S_n$.

5. What is the geometrical interpretation of the derivative?

   Geometrically, the integral of a function is the area under a function's curve.

6. What was the long (but thorough) way of finding derivatives?

   The long way of finding derivatives is the Method of Increments.

7. What was the long (but thorough) way of finding integrals?

   The long way of finding integrals is the Method of Summation.

8. What is the shortcut method for finding the derivative of power functions and their sums? Write it out in symbolic form.

   The shortcut method for finding the derivative of power functions and their sums is the Power Rule. The Power Rule is: for any power function $f(x)=Kx^n$, its derivative is $f'(x)=nKx^{n-1}$.

9. What rule did we use to calculate anti-derivatives of power functions (and their sums)? Write it out in symbolic form.

   The rule we used to calculate anti-derivatives of power functions is called the Reverse Power Rule. The Reverse Power Rule is: for any power function $f(x) = Kx^n$ when $x \neq -1$, its anti-derivative is $F(x) = \frac{K}{n+1}x^{n+1}$.

10. What is the generic form of a power function? How do the shortcut methods effect the exponent on this generic form?

    The generic from of a power function is $f(x)=Kx^n$. The Power Rule reduces the exponent by 1, giving us n-1. The Reverse Power Rule increases the exponent by 1, giving us n+1.

11. In symbolic form (and in terms of $F(x)$) what is the formula that says the derivative of the anti-derivative is the original function $f(x)$?

    The formula that says the derivative of the anti-derivative is the original function is $\frac{d}{dx}\left[F(x)\right] = f(x)$.

12. In words, what does the Fundamental Theorem of Calculus tell us?

    The Fundamental Theorem of Calculus tells us that the antiderivative is the same this as the integral.

13. In symbols, what is the Fundamental Theorem of Calculus?

    In symbols, the Fundamental Theorem of Calculus is $\int_a^b f(x)dx = F(x)\Big|_a^b = F(b) - F(a)$.

14. What is our new shorthand way of representing $F(b)$-$F(a)$?

    Our new shorthand way of representing is $F(b) - F(a)$ is $F(x)\Big|_a^b$.

15. What are the three main steps in using the Fundamental Theorem to calculate integrals?

    The three main steps in using the Fundamental Theorem of Calculus to calculate integrals are: $\int_a^b F(x)$ at the two x-values a and b, that is, evaluate $F(a)$ and $F(b)$. Third, subtract $F(a)$ from $F(b)$.

16. Just as we can take the derivative of the anti-derivative of $f(x)$ to return to the original function $f(x)$, we can get the original function $f(x)$ by taking the derivative of the integral of $f(x)$. How did we put this in symbolic form?

    We can get the original function by taking the derivative of the integral of . In symbols this is $\frac{d}{dx}(\int f(x)dx) = f(x)$.

17. How is the Fundamental theorem practically helpful?

    The Fundamental Theorem is practically helpful because it simplifies the evaluation of integrals, but more than that, it makes many evaluations *possible*. If we want to calculate integrals exactly, the Fundamental Theorem often provides the only way.

18. How is the Fundamental theorem helpful for the theory of calculus?

    The Fundamental Theorem is helpful for the theory of calculus because prior to the discovery of the Fundamental Theorem, calculus wasn't really a *single* thing. The Fundamental Theorem of Calculus takes the various parts of calculus (i.e. differentiation and integration) and brings them together.

19. What are the two kinds of integrals we discussed in the chapter?

    The two kinds of integrals we discussed are the definite integral and the indefinite integral.

20. How is the definite integral interpreted in geometrical terms? Why is it called "definite"? Is the definite integral a number or a function? In symbols what is the definite integral?

    In geometrical terms, the definite integral is an area. It's called "definite" because it has a specific boundary or limit. The definite integral gives us a finite, single numerical value. In symbols, the definite integral is $\int_a^b f(x)dx$.

21. Why is the indefinite integral called "indefinite"? Is the indefinite integral a number or a function? In symbols, what is the indefinite integral?

    The indefinite integral is called "indefinite" because there are no upper and lower limits. The indefinite integral is a generic function. In symbols, the indefinite integral is $\int f(x)dx$.

22. Calculus is sometimes divided into two main kinds. What are they?

    Calculus is sometimes divided into differential calculus and integral calculus.

23. What does "integrate" mean, generally?

    "Integrate" generally means "collecting individual things into a single whole" or "putting things together."

24. What does "integrate" have to do with the Method of *Summation*?

    In the Method of Summation, we added together the areas of mini-rectangles. This "adding together" is what connects "integrate" and the Method of Summation.

25. What was the Latin phrase with which Leibniz referred to the part of calculus that dealt with integration? What does this mean in English? How does the integral symbol help you remember this?

    The Latin phrase which Leibniz used to refer to the part of calculus that dealt with integration was *calculus summatorius*. In English this means "calculus of summation." The integral symbol helps us to remember this because it is a long *s*.

26. What was the Latin phrase with which Leibniz referred to the part of calculus that dealt with differentiation? What does this mean in English?

    The Latin phrase which Leibniz used to refer to the part of calculus that dealt with differentiation was *calculus differentialis*. In English this means "differential calculus" or "calculus of differentials."

27. What is a *differential*? How do we represent differentials symbolically? How is this related to the concept of "difference"?

    A *differential* is an infinitely small change like and . We represent differentials with the symbol . This is related to the concept of "difference" because a differential is the infinitesimal *difference* between two values.

28. Why do we tend to use Leibniz's notation and terms rather than Newton's?

    We tend to use Leibniz's notation and terms rather than Newton's because Leibniz was the first to publish his findings. Also, Leibniz was concerned with making

calculus clear and easy to understand, whereas Newton was more interested in simply using the tool to help him solve problems he himself was working on.

29. What does "derive" mean?

    "To derive" means "to use reason to arrive at something new" or "to flow out of."

30. What terms did Newton use for integrals and derivatives?

    Newton used the terms *fluent* and *fluxion* to denote integrals and derivatives.

31. What does the word *calculus* mean?

    The Latin word *calculus* means "pebble" and since pebbles or stones were used to count and study the properties of numbers, we get the association with our word "calculate." Leibniz's use of *calculus* narrowed the term to the topic we're studying in this book.

EXERCISE SOLUTIONS

1) $A=\int_1^3 4x\,dx=\frac{4}{2}x^2+C\Big|_1^3=2x^2+C\Big|_1^2=\left[2(3)^2+C\right]-\left[\left(2(1)^2+C\right)\right]=$
$=18+C-2-C=16$

2) $A=\int_0^2 x^2dx=\frac{1}{3}x^3+C\Big|_0^2=\left[\frac{1}{3}(2)^3+C\right]-\left[\frac{1}{3}(0)^3+C\right]=$
$=\frac{8}{3}+C-0-C=\frac{8}{3}$

3) a. $\int_1^3 6x^3dx=\frac{6}{4}x^4+C\Big|_1^3=\left[\frac{3}{2}(3)^4+C\right]-\left[\frac{3}{2}(1)^4+C\right]=$
$=\frac{3(81)}{2}+C-\frac{3}{2}-C=\frac{243}{2}-\frac{3}{2}=\frac{240}{2}=120$

b. $\int_1^2 x^4dx=\frac{1}{5}x^5+C\Big|_1^2=\left[\frac{1}{5}(2)^5+C\right]-\left[\frac{1}{5}(1)^5+C\right]=$
$=\frac{32}{5}+C-\frac{1}{5}-C=\frac{31}{5}$

c. $\int_0^1 (3x^6 + x^4 + 3x)\,dx = \frac{3}{7}x^7 + \frac{1}{5}x^5 + \frac{3}{2}x^2 + C\Big|_0^1 =$

$$= \left[\frac{3}{7}(1)^7 + \frac{1}{5}(1)^5 + \frac{3}{2}(1)^2 + C\right] - \left[\frac{3}{7}(0)^7 + \frac{1}{5}(0)^5 + \frac{3}{2}(0)^2 + C\right]$$

$$= \frac{3}{7} + \frac{1}{5} + \frac{3}{2} + C - 0 - 0 - 0 - C = \frac{30}{70} + \frac{14}{70} + \frac{105}{70} = \frac{149}{70}$$

4) a. $\int x^2 dx = \frac{1}{3}x^3 + C$

b. $\int x^{99} dx = \frac{1}{100}x^{100} + C$

c. $\int (5x^7 + 5x^5)dx = \frac{5}{8}x^8 + \frac{5}{6}x^6 + C$

d. $\int \left[-\frac{3\sqrt{x}}{7}\right]dx = \int \left[-\frac{3}{7}x^{\frac{1}{2}}\right]dx = -\frac{3}{7}\cdot\frac{1}{\left[\frac{1}{2}+\frac{2}{2}\right]}x^{\frac{1}{2}+\frac{2}{3}} + C =$

$$= -\frac{3}{7\cdot\frac{3}{2}}x^{\frac{3}{2}} + C = -\frac{2}{7}x^{\frac{3}{2}} + C = -\frac{2}{7}\sqrt{x^3} + C$$

e. $\int \left[9x^7 - \pi\sqrt[3]{x} + \frac{1}{\sqrt{x}} + x\right]dx = \int \left[9x^7 - \pi x^{\frac{1}{3}} + x^{-\frac{1}{2}} + x\right]dx =$

$$= \frac{9}{8}x^8 - \frac{\pi}{\left[\frac{1}{3}+\frac{3}{3}\right]}x^{\frac{1}{3}+\frac{3}{3}} + \frac{1}{\left[-\frac{1}{2}+\frac{2}{2}\right]}x^{-\frac{1}{2}+\frac{2}{2}} + \frac{1}{2}x^2 + C =$$

$$= \frac{9}{8}x^8 - \frac{\pi}{\frac{4}{3}}x^{\frac{4}{3}} + \frac{1}{\frac{1}{2}}x^{\frac{1}{2}} + \frac{1}{2}x^2 + C =$$

$$= \frac{9}{8}x^8 - \frac{3\pi}{4}x^{\frac{4}{3}} + 2x^{\frac{1}{2}} + \frac{1}{2}x^2 + C =$$

$$= \frac{9}{8}x^8 - \frac{3\pi}{4}\sqrt[3]{x^4} + 2\sqrt{x} + \frac{1}{2}x^2 + C$$

f. $\int (ax^n)dx = \frac{a}{n+1}x^{n+1} + C$

g. $\int \left[\frac{a}{n+1}x^{n+1} + C\right]dx = \frac{a}{n+1}\cdot\frac{1}{(n+1)+1}x^{(n+1)+1} + Cx + C_2 = \frac{a}{n+1}\cdot\frac{1}{n+2}x^{n+2} +$

$$+ Cx + C_2 = \frac{a}{(n+1)(n+2)}x^{n+2} + Cx + C_2 = \frac{a}{n^2 + 2n + n + 2}x^{n+2} + Cx + C_2$$

$$= \frac{a}{n^2 + 3n + 2}x^{n+2} + Cx + C_2$$

5) We know that for *any* free fall scenario that $a(t) = -32$ and that $v(t) = A(t) = \int(-32)\,dt = -32t + C$.

In *this* particular case, we're told that $v(0) = 0$ (because the object is simply dropped) and so

$$v_0 = v(0) = 0 = -32(0) + C \quad \Rightarrow \quad C = 0$$

This gives us

$$v(t) = -32t.$$

Now,

$$h(t) = v(t) = \int -32t\,dt = -\frac{32}{2}t^2 + C = -16t^2 + C,$$

where,

$$h(0) = 100 = -16(0)^2 + C \quad \Rightarrow \quad C = 100$$

and so

$$h(t) = -16t^2 + 100.$$

6) $a(t) = -32$

$$v(t) = A(t) = \int(-32)\,dt = -32t + C$$
$$v(0) = 30 = -32(0) + C \quad \Rightarrow \quad C = 30$$
$$v(t) = -32t + 30$$

$$h(t) = v(t) = \int(-32t + 30)\,dt = -\frac{32}{2}t^2 + 30t + C = -16t^2 + 30t + C$$
$$h(0) = 4 = -16(0)^2 + 30(0) + C \quad \Rightarrow \quad C = 4$$
$$h(t) = -16t^2 + 30t + 4$$

CHAPTER 25 - INTERPRETING AREAS

ANSWERS TO THE STUDY QUESTIONS

1. What is one of the main themes of this book? What is (or should be) surprising about this?

   One of the main themes of this book is the applicability of mathematics to the physical world. What should be surprising about this is that we can do Math in our heads and on paper and it can give us truths about the physical world.

2. What geometrical property is the derivative associated with? What physical quantities can this geometrical property be associated with?

   Geometrically, the derivative is associated with the slope of a function. This geometrical property, slope, can be associated with the physical properties of speed and acceleration.

3. What geometrical property is the integral associated with? What physical quantities can this geometrical property be associated with? Why didn't I talk about this earlier when introducing integrals?

   Geometrically, the integral is associated with areas, specifically, the areas under a function's curve. This geometrical property, area, can be associated with the physical properties of "change in velocity" and "change in height." We didn't talk about the physical association of this geometrical property earlier because we didn't have a relatively simple method to calculate integrals, not until we explored the Fundamental Theorem of Calculus.

4. What physical property is represented by the area "under" the acceleration curve?

   The physical property represented by the area "under" the acceleration curve is "change in velocity."

5. What physical property is represented by the area "under" the velocity curve?

   The physical property represented by the area "under" the velocity curve is "change in distance" or "change in height" in the case of free fall.

EXERCISE SOLUTIONS

1) $h(t) = -16t + 100 \Rightarrow$ 100 is the initial height, h_0, and there is no initial velocity, v_0 and so
$v(t) = -32t$ & $a(t) = -32$

Let's try to solve the problem without looking at a graph. To find the change in velocity, Δh, between 1 s and 2 s, we take the integral of the acceleration curve (a definite integral in this case). That is, we find the area "under" the acceleration curve (let's call it A_a for "area under acceleration curve"):

$$\Delta v = A_a = \int_1^2 -32\,\mathrm{dt} = -32t + C\Big|_1^2 = -32(2) + C - \big[-32(1) + C\big] =$$
$$= -64 + 32 = -32\ \frac{\text{ft}}{\text{s}}$$

So, between 1 second and 2 seconds, the speed changes (increases!) by 32 ft/s, but in the downward direction, due to the negative sign.

To find the change in height, Δh, well take the integral of $v(t)$ over the interval between 1 and 2 seconds. That is, we find the area "under" the velocity curve (let's call it A_v for "area under velocity curve"):

$$\Delta h = A_v = \int_1^2 -32t\,dt = -16t^2 + C\Big|_1^2 = -16(2)^2 + C - \big[-16(1)^2 + C\big] = -64 + 16 =$$
$$= -48\,\text{ft}$$

So, the object's height changed 48 ft in the negative direction. That is, it *fell* 48 ft.

2) To find the change in velocity we take the following integral (finding the area under the acceleration curve):

$$\Delta v = A_a = \int_0^{2.03} -32\,dt = \ 32t + C\Big|_0^{2.03} = -32(2.03) + C - \big[-32(0) + C\big] =$$
$$= -64.96\ \text{ft/s}$$

We know from the graph & formulas that the initial speed, v_0, is 30 ft/s in the upward direction. The object will slow down and eventually stop at its highest point. When it has stopped at this apex, the change in speed will have been –30 ft/s. In this case, because the object is traveling upward, the negative sign means that it slowed down, its speed decreased by 30 ft/s. But on its *downward* trajectory, the object's speed increases a total of 34.96 ft/s in the downward direction. The total change in speed, given the coordinate system, is –64.96 ft/s. Notice that we need to take into account the both the direction of the object *and* whether the numerical values are positive or negative. Negative signs mean different things for objects moving in different directions. It's not difficult, but it requires attention to detail and careful accounting. Safety first!

For the change in height we take the definite integral of the velocity curve, finding the area between the curve and horizontal axis from 0 to 2.03 s. But we are looking for the *net* area, so we'll be "adding" the two areas, the one above—and the one below—the horizontal axis. Let's call the triangular area that is above the horizontal axis, A_{above}, and the area below the horizontal axis, A_{below}.

$$\Delta h = A_v = A_{above} + A_{below} = \underbrace{\int_0^{.938} (-32t+30)\,dt}_{A_{above}} + \underbrace{\int_{.938}^{2.03} (-32t+30)\,dt}_{A_{below}}$$

Let's calculate each area separately:

$$A_{above} = (-16t^2+30t+C)\Big|_0^{.938} = -16(.938)^2+30(.938)+C- \\ -\left[-16(0)^2+30(0)+C\right] = -14.08+28.14+C-\left[0+0+C\right] = 14.06\text{ ft}$$

$$A_{below} = (-16t^2+30t)\Big|_{.938}^{2.03} = -16(2.03)^2+30(2.03)-\left[-16(.938)^2+30(.938)\right] = \\ = -65.93+60.9-(-14.08+28.14) = -5.03-14.06 = -19.09\text{ ft}$$

$$\Delta h = A_v = A_{above} + A_{below} = 14.06\text{ ft} - 19.09\text{ ft} = -5.03\text{ ft}$$

So, according to this calculation, the net or overall change in height is –5.03 ft. In other words, the object ends up 5.03 ft *below* where it started. But look again at the graph (& the height formula):

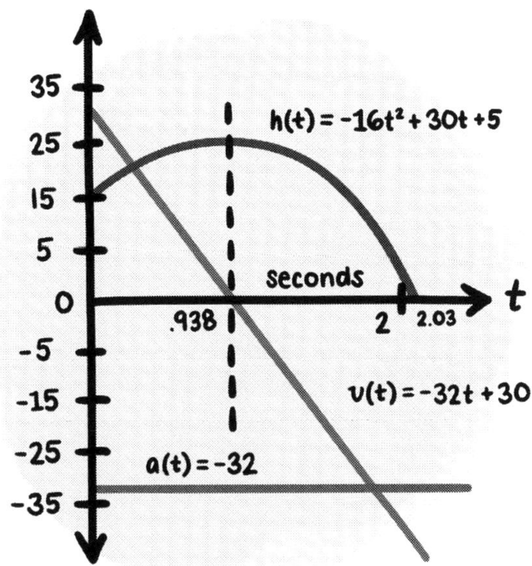

The *net* change in height should be 5 ft *exactly*, since the object began 5 ft above the ground and ended at ground level which is defined as 0 ft. So what happened? Why 5.03 ft instead of 5 ft exactly?

This is a great example of why the number of digits after the decimal matter in calculations. The endpoint time that I gave you for when the object hits the ground was 2.03 s, but technically it's more like 2.029015575 s! If you do the calculations with this more precise number, the Δh is much closer to exactly 5 ft.

3) This exercise is asking you to make a very general calculation, one that represents any beginning time and any ending time. As usual,

$$h(t) = -16t^2 + v_0 t + h_0 \quad \Rightarrow \quad v(t) = -32t + v_0 \quad \Rightarrow \quad a(t) = -32$$

The change in speed, Δv, is given by the area "under" the acceleration curve (let's again call it A_a, where the subscript a stands for 'acceleration' and not for the beginning time, which we also called a).

$$\Delta v = A_a = \int_a^b -32\,dt = -32t\Big| + C_a^b = -32(b) + C - \left[-32(a) + C\right] =$$
$$= -32 \cdot b + 32 \cdot a = -32(b - a)$$

The change in the height, Δh, is given by the area "under" the velocity curve (let's call it A_v):

$$\Delta h = A_v = \int_a^b (-32t + v_0)\,dt = -16t^2 + v_0 t + C\Big|_a^b =$$
$$= -16(b)^2 + v_0(b) + C - \left[-16(a)^2 + v_0(a) + C\right] =$$
$$= -16b^2 + v_0 b + 16a^2 - v_0 a =$$
$$= -16(b^2 - a^2) + v_0(b - a)$$

4) Using the result from the previous exercise, check exercise (1) where a = 1 and b = 2:

$$\Delta v = A_a = -32(b - a) =$$
$$= -32(2 - 1) =$$
$$= -32(1) =$$
$$= -32 \text{ ft/s}$$
$$\Delta h = A_v = -16(b^2 - a^2) + v_0(b - a) =$$
$$= -16(2^2 - 1^2) + 0(2 - 1) =$$
$$= -16(4 - 1) =$$
$$= -16(3) =$$
$$= -48 \text{ ft}$$

Now let's check exercise (2), where a = 0 and b = 2.03

$$\Delta v = A_a = -32(b - a) =$$
$$= -32(2.03 - 0) =$$
$$= -32 \cdot 2.03 =$$
$$= -64.96 \text{ ft/s}$$
$$\Delta h = A_v = -16(b^2 - a^2) + v_0(b - a) =$$
$$= -16(2.03^2 - 0^2) + 30(2.03 - 0) =$$
$$= -16 \cdot 2.03^2 + 30 \cdot 2.03 =$$
$$= -65.95 + 60.9 =$$
$$= -5.03 \text{ ft}$$

EPILOGUE: THE PROBLEM OF CHANGE

ANSWERS TO THE STUDY QUESTIONS

1. What is an epilogue?

   An epilogue is a conclusion. In this book, the epilogue serves to put a final coat of paint on all we've learned.

2. One last time, what are the three central concepts in calculus? What ties them all together?

   The three central concepts in in calculus are the limit, derivative, and integral of a function. The Fundamental Theorem of Calculus ties them all together.

3. What problem was calculus ultimately invented to solve? With whom did that problem begin? Who turned it into a mathematical problem?

   Calculus was ultimately invented to solve the problem of change. The problem began with Thales in ancient Greece. Plato and the Pythagoreans turned the problem of change into a mathematical problem.

4. What was the name of Newton's great work on mathematical physics? What year was it published?

   Newton's great work on mathematical physics is called ***The Mathematical Principles of Natural Philosophy*****, or in Latin,** ***Philosophiae Naturalis Principia Mathematica*****. Newton's work was published in 1687.**

5. What were the three Pythagorean ideas that were at the foundation of the Scientific Revolution?

   The three Pythagorean ideas that were at the foundation of the Scientific Revolution were that the universe is ordered according to perfect mathematical laws, that divine reason is the orderer, and that human reason can discern the divine mathematical pattern.

6. What two theories replaced Newtonian physics in the early 1900s?

General relativity and quantum mechanics replaced Newtonian physics in the early 1900's.

7. Explain how mathematics acts as a kind of seeing-eye dog.

   Mathematics acts as a kind of seeing-eye dog by telling us truths about things we cannot directly observe. For example, one physicist found that his calculations resulted in the prediction of a subatomic particle that had a negative energy, and a later physicist, Paul Dirac, won the Nobel Prize for discovering antimatter.

8. How much of the universe is made up of galaxies, nebulae, stars, planets, and humans?

   Only five percent of the universe is made up of galaxies, nebulae, stars, planets, and humans.

9. Why are physicists trying to find a replacement for general relativity and quantum mechanics?

   Physicists are trying to find a replacement for general relativity and quantum mechanics because the two theories contradict one another where they overlap.

10. At present, what is the leading candidate for a theory of everything? Why would the Pythagoreans be pleased? What is the downside to this theory?

    The leading candidate for a theory of everything is superstring theory (or just string theory). The Pythagoreans would be pleased with this theory because they were the ones who began the whole endeavor of mathematical physics by discovering that a vibrating string could be described with numbers. The downside of string theory is that there is no known way to make observations to support it.

11. What concept of calculus did we use to solve Zeno's paradox?

    We used the concept of limits to solve Zeno's paradox.

12. Essay: How would you explain to someone who hasn't taken this class that "Calculus is for everyone"?

    See the final paragraph of the epilogue for ideas that should be included in an essay explaining why "Calculus is for everyone."

EXERCISE SOLUTIONS

1) Zeros paradox can be mathematically formulated by noting that the progressive dividing in half of the total distance (say, one mile) can be written as follows:

$$\text{Sum} = \frac{1}{2} + \frac{1}{4} + \frac{1}{8} + \frac{1}{16} + \cdots$$

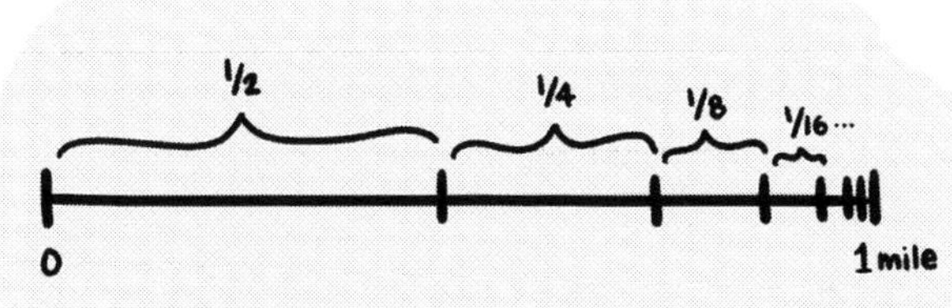

We can write the above sum in terms of n number of divisions (let's call this definite sum, Sum_n):

$$\begin{aligned}\text{Sum}_n &= \frac{1}{2} + \frac{1}{4} + \frac{1}{8} + \frac{1}{16} + \cdots + \frac{1}{2^n} = \\ &= \frac{1}{2^1} + \frac{1}{2^2} + \frac{1}{2^3} + \frac{1}{2^4} + \cdots + \frac{1}{2^n}\end{aligned}$$

To get rid of the "..." we note the simple and obvious fact (though it's not obvious at first *why* we would do this) that

$$\text{Sum}_n = \frac{1}{2}\text{Sum}_n + \frac{1}{2}\text{Sum}_n.$$

This can be rearranged as follows (though again, it might not be entirely clear at this stage why we would do this):

$$\text{Sum}_n - \frac{1}{2}\text{Sum}_n = \frac{1}{2}\text{Sum}_n.$$

Let's now write this subtraction problem vertically:

$$\begin{array}{l}\text{Sum}_n \\ -\frac{1}{2}\text{Sum}_n \\ \hline \frac{1}{2}\text{Sum}_n\end{array}$$

And $\frac{1}{2}\text{Sum}_n$ is equal to

$$
\begin{aligned}
\frac{1}{2}\text{Sum}_n &= \frac{1}{2}\cdot\left[\frac{1}{2^1}+\frac{1}{2^2}+\frac{1}{2^3}+\frac{1}{2^4}+\cdots+\frac{1}{2^n}\right] \\
&= \frac{1}{2^1\cdot 2^1}+\frac{1}{2^1\cdot 2^2}+\frac{1}{2^1\cdot 2^3}+\frac{1}{2^1\cdot 2^4}+\cdots+\frac{1}{2^1\cdot 2^n} \\
&= \frac{1}{2^{1+1}}+\frac{1}{2^{2+1}}+\frac{1}{2^{3+1}}+\frac{1}{2^{4+1}}+\cdots+\frac{1}{2^{n+1}} \\
&= \frac{1}{2^2}+\frac{1}{2^3}+\frac{1}{2^4}+\frac{1}{2^5}+\cdots+\frac{1}{2^{n+1}}
\end{aligned}
$$

Plugging this result into the vertical subtraction problem:

$$
\begin{aligned}
\text{Sum}_n &= \frac{1}{2^1}+\cancel{\frac{1}{2^2}}+\cancel{\frac{1}{2^3}}+\cancel{\frac{1}{2^4}}+\cancel{\frac{1}{2^5}}+\cdots+\cancel{\frac{1}{2^n}} \\
-\frac{1}{2}\text{Sum}_n &= \cancel{\frac{1}{2^2}}+\cancel{\frac{1}{2^3}}+\cancel{\frac{1}{2^4}}+\cancel{\frac{1}{2^5}}+\cdots\cancel{\frac{1}{2^n}}+\frac{1}{2^{n+1}} \\
\hline
\frac{1}{2}\text{Sum}_n &= \frac{1}{2}-\frac{1}{2^{n+1}}
\end{aligned}
$$

Taking this answer to the subtraction problem, solve for Sum_n (the algebra is carried out in a slightly different order than in the chapter but it's entirely equivalent):

$$
\begin{aligned}
\text{Sum} &= 2\left[\frac{1}{2}-\frac{1}{2^{\ +1}}\right] \\
&= \frac{2}{2}-\frac{2}{2^{\ +1}} \\
&= 1-\frac{1}{2^{\ +1-1}} \\
&= 1-\frac{1}{2^n}
\end{aligned}
$$

The total distance, then, is

$$
\lim_{n\to\infty}\left[1-\frac{1}{2^n}\right]=1\,\text{mile}
$$

And so the total distance is traversed.

ANSWER KEY FOR EXAMS

Printable blank exams may be downloaded at
RomanRoadsPress.com/Materials

CALCULUS FOR EVERYONE

EXAM 1: ANSWER KEY

CHAPTERS 1-8

1. There were two main ways in which Thales was important. What are they?

   The two main ways in which Thales was important are: first, he set the agenda for Western philosophy with his attempt to explain why the world around us changes while maintaining so much order; and second, he was the first mathematician (the first person to try to systematically prove mathematical statements).

2. What was the Pythagorean motto? Explain what this motto means. (Hint: How did Morris Kline unpack the motto?)

   The Pythagorean motto was "All is number." This motto has three underlying ideas: first, that the universe is ordered according to perfect mathematical laws; second, that divine reason is the orderer; and third, that human reason can discern the divine mathematical pattern.

3. What did Wigner say about the applicability of mathematics to the physical world? Why couldn't he make sense of why math "works"? How did Plato make sense of it?

   Wigner said that "The miracle of the appropriateness of the language of mathematics for the formulation of the laws of physics is a wonderful gift which we neither understand nor deserve." In other words, he said we cannot understand why math "works." He couldn't make sense of why math "works" because he was not aware that the universe was created by an intelligent designer, a God who is a mathematician. Plato made sense of the applicability of math by saying that the world *is* mathematical, and he believed that the world was mathematical because God made it that way.

4. Explain how Plato's *Republic* is important in the history of the liberal arts. What does this have to do with Pythagoras?

   The education that Plato sketches in his book the *Republic* is where the West gets the notion of the liberal arts. There are seven liberal arts and four of them, the *quadrivium* (arithmetic, geometry, astronomy, and music) were handed down to Plato by the Pythagoreans.

5. What is Plato's challenge?

   Plato's challenge is to mathematically describe the apparently chaotic motion of the heavens.

6. What was Zeno's outrageous suggestion? What was his argument for this?

   Zeno's outrageous suggestion was that motion simply can't occur. He argued that, in order to traverse any distance, you would first have to traverse half of it. But to traverse half the distance, you would first need to traverse half of that distance (a quarter of the original distance). Zeno said that we could continue dividing distances forever, meaning that we would need to travers an infinite number of distances which would take an infinite amount of time—an eternity. Since traversing any distance would mean traversing an infinite number of distances in an infinite amount of time, Zeno concluded that motion was impossible.

7. How are mathematical lines and physical distance in space different? How are they alike? Why are their similarities important?

   Mathematical lines and physical distance in space are different because mathematical lines are mathematical objccts, not physical ones, whereas physical distance is physical. We take the similarity between mathematical lines and physical distance for granted, so much so that we do not question when a line is used to represent distance. The similarity between mathematical lines and physical distance is important because it allows us to use mathematics in science.

8. What two realms does the number line unite?

   The number line unites the realm of numbers and the realm of points.

9. What is the paradox of speed? Make sure to express it in words as well as in Δ notation.

   The paradox of speed is that instantaneous speed doesn't seem to make any sense. When we consider an object changing location, it seems that it is moving at every moment in time, at every instant. However, in an instant of time, no time passes, and if no time passes, then no distance can be traveled. The paradox is that in any given instant, no motion occurs, but this does not fit with our observations. We can express this in Δ notation this way:

$$v_{ave} = \frac{\Delta x}{\Delta t} = \frac{0}{0}$$

   Here we see another problem. We have a zero in the denominator which is undefined or meaningless.

10. What do *we* say causes a dropped ball to fall? What does Aristotle say the cause is? In each case, *where* are these causes?

    We say that gravity causes a dropped ball to fall. Aristotle says that the ball's nature causes it to fall. Gravity is an external cause whereas Aristotle's answer made the cause internal.

11. What does the Greek word *physis* mean? What word do we derive from it?

    The Greek word *physis* means nature, and it is the source of our word *physics*.

12. What is the "principle of change"?

    Aristotle said that the principle of change is an object's nature.

13. Write out, in words, Archimedes' Law of the Lever. Draw a diagram for this, label it, and write out as a formula.

    Archimedes' Law of the Lever is this: "Two magnitudes balance at distances reciprocally proportional to the magnitudes."

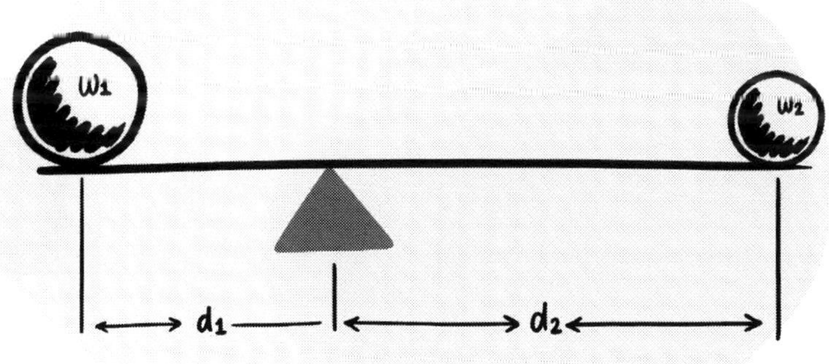

$$w_1 \cdot d_1 = w_2 \cdot d_2$$

$$\frac{w_1}{w_2} = \frac{d_2}{d_1}$$

14. Why is the Scientific Revolution called a "revolution"? What is it called a "scientific" revolution?

    The Scientific Revolution is called a "revolution" because it overthrew the existing regime. It is called a "scientific" revolution because it overthrew the *scientific* regime of Aristotle.

15. How might we characterize the Scientific Revolution in terms of the Platonic-Pythagorean tradition?

    We might say, as the eminent historian of science Richard Westfall did, that the Scientific Revolution was dominated or characterized by the resurgence of the Platonic-Pythagorean tradition, which looked on nature in geometric terms, convinced that the cosmos was constructed according to the principles of mathematical order.

16. In summary, what are the three main results of the Scientific Revolution? What is a fourth?

    The three main results of the Scientific Revolution are: first, the overthrow of Aristotle; second, the reintroduction of the Platonic-Pythagorean project; and third, the mathematization of motion. A fourth result of the Scientific Revolution is the development of the mechanical philosophy, the philosophy that views the universe like a machine (e.g. a clock) as opposed to Aristotle's philosophy which viewed the world more like a living organism.

17. Turn Galileo's law of fall (notice that we have a ratio)

$$\frac{d_1}{d_2} = \frac{t_1^2}{t_2^2}$$

into

$$\frac{v_{ave,1}}{v_{ave,2}} = \frac{t_1}{t_2}$$

Answer:

$$d = v_{ave} \cdot t \Rightarrow v_{ave} = \frac{d}{t} \Rightarrow \frac{d_1}{d_2} = \frac{t_1^2}{t_2^2} = \frac{t_1 \cdot t_1}{t_2 \cdot t_2} \Rightarrow \frac{d_1}{t_1} \cdot \frac{t_2}{d_2} = \frac{t_1}{t_2}$$

$$\Rightarrow v_{ave,1} \cdot \frac{1}{v_{ave,2}} = \frac{t_1}{t_2} \Rightarrow \frac{v_{ave,1}}{v_{ave,2}} = \frac{t_1}{t_2}$$

18. What was Galileo's view on cosmology?

Galileo had a Copernican or heliocentric view of cosmology.

19. What is the full name of Newton's *Principia* (in English)? In what year was it first published? How is unifying physics related to Newton's *Principia*? How is this related to the problem of change and calculus?

The full English name of Newton's *Principia* is *The Mathematical Principles of Natural Philosophy*. It was first published in 1687. In his work, Newton derived a set of mathematical laws that applied to the entire cosmos, in other words, he derived a set of mathematical laws that unified physics. The mathematical principles required calculus and were a major leap in solving the mathematized problem of change set by the Pythagoreans and Plato.

20. What are the three Pythagorean theses that Morris Kline said were the core beliefs underlying the Scientifict Revolution?

    The three Pythagorean theses that Morris Kline said were the core beliefs underlying the Scientific Revolution are:

    1. **The universe is ordered according to perfect mathematical laws**
    2. **Divine reason is the orderer**
    3. **Human reason can discern the divine mathematical pattern**

21. Very briefly—in a single sentence—what is calculus?

    Calculus is the mathematics of change.

22. What were the four main problems that calculus was invented to solve?

    The four main problems that calculus was invented to solve were:

    1. **Describing continually changing velocity and acceleration**
    2. **Finding the slope of a curve (including minimum and maximum values)**
    3. **Finding the tangent line to a curve**
    4. **Finding the area under a curve**

23. What does it mean to *quantify* a property?

    To quantify a property means to represent a physical property with numbers.

24. What is a function?

A function is a relation between variables.

25. What is a graph and why is it useful?

A graph is a picture of a function, it *shows* how variables behave together. It is useful because sometimes it is much easier to *see* how variables behave than to have their behavior described in words or formulas.

26. What is analytic geometry?

Analytic geometry is a mathematical system that combines algebraic formulas with pictures in Cartesian coordinates. In other words, analytic geometry is the algebraic representation of shapes and the geometrical representation of algebraic formulas.

27. What are the three main concepts of calculus? What law tells us that all of them are related?

The three main concepts of calculus are:

1. **The limit of a function**
2. **The derivative of a function**
3. **The integral of a function**

28. Finish the sentence, "limit = the value you approach but ___________." Why does this make the "method of substitution" somewhat misleading? Make sure you know who Tantalus is.

"Limit = the value you approach but never reach." This makes the method of substitution somewhat misleading because this method can make it look as if we're allowing our input value to equal the forbidden value when we can really only approach the forbidden value.

29. How does the metaphor of standing versus seeing help explain why limits are exact even though they are only approached but never reached?

The metaphor of standing versus seeing helps explain why limits are exact even though they are only approached but never reached because we understand that you do not need to stand on a gap to know exactly where it is. Instead, if you can get close to the gap, you can see exactly where it is, even without standing directly on it.

30. Evaluate the following (if there is a value that the variable cannot be, make sure to note it):

a. $\lim_{x \to 0} (x^2+2)$

Answer:

$$\lim_{x \to 0}\left(x^2+2\right)=0+2=2$$

b. $\lim_{x \to 3} \left(\frac{x^2 - 9}{x - 3} \right)$

Answer:

$$\frac{x^2-9}{x-3} = \frac{(x+3)\cancel{(x-3)}}{\cancel{x-3}} = x+3 \quad \Rightarrow \quad \lim_{x \to 3}\left[\frac{x^2-9}{x-3}\right] = \lim_{x \to 3}(x+3) = 6$$

$(x \neq 3)$

c. $\lim_{x \to 4} \left(\frac{x - 4}{x^2 - x - 12} \right)$

Answer:

$$\frac{x-4}{x^2-x-12} = \frac{\cancel{x-4}}{(\cancel{x-4})(x+3)} = \frac{1}{x+3} \quad \Rightarrow \quad \lim_{x \to 4}\left[\frac{x-4}{x^2-x-12}\right]$$

$$\Rightarrow \lim_{x \to 4}\left[\frac{1}{x+3}\right] = \frac{1}{7} \qquad (x \neq 4 \text{ or} -3)$$

d. $\lim_{x \to 0} \left(\frac{x^3}{x} \right)$

Answer:

$$\lim_{x \to 0}\left[\frac{x^3}{x}\right] = \lim_{x \to 0}\left(x^2\right) = 0 \qquad (x \neq 0)$$

CALCULUS FOR EVERYONE

EXAM 2: ANSWER KEY

CHAPTERS 9-14

---

1. Write the definition of average speed in delta notaion.

$$v_{ave} = \frac{\Delta d}{\Delta t}$$

2. What is acceleration?

Acceleration means that a speed is not constant, or that the speed is changing.

3. In words, describe the method of approximation for finding (i.e., approximating) instantaneous speed at some particular instant.

Using the method of approximation, we can find the instantaneous speed at some particular instant by calculating the average speed over smaller and smaller time intervals near the particular instant. As the time interval approaches 0 seconds, the average velocity approaches the instantaneous velocity at the particular instant.

4. Define instantaneous speed/velocity in symbols.

$$v = \lim_{\Delta t \to 0} (v_{ave}) = \lim_{\Delta t \to 0} \left(\frac{\Delta d}{\Delta t} \right)$$

5. Using the method of approximation, find the instantaneous speed of a falling object after it has fallen 2 seconds. Also calculate how far it has fallen during that time.

$$v_{ave} = \frac{\Delta d}{\Delta t} = \frac{d(2)-d(1.75)}{2-1.75} = \frac{16(2)^2-16(1.75)^2}{.25} = \frac{64-49}{.25} = 60 \text{ ft/s}$$
$$v_{ave} = \frac{d(2)-d(1.9)}{2-1.9} = \frac{16(2)^2-16(1.9)^2}{.1} = \frac{64-57.6}{.1} = 62.4 \text{ ft/s}$$
$$v_{ave} = \frac{d(2)-d(1.99)}{2-1.99} = \frac{16(2)^2-16(1.99)^2}{.01} = \frac{64-63.36}{.01} = 63.84 \text{ ft/s}$$
$$v_{ave} = \frac{d(2)-d(1.999)}{2-1.999} = \frac{16(2)^2-16(1.999)^2}{.001} = \frac{64-63.936}{.001} = 63.984 \text{ ft/s}$$
$$v_{ave} = \frac{d(2)-d(1.9999)}{2-1.9999} = \frac{16(2)^2-16(1.9999)^2}{.0001} = \frac{64-63.994}{.0001} = 64.00 \text{ ft/s}$$

Approaching 64 ft/s.

$d = 16(2)^2 = 64$ ft

6. What are the two steps of the Method of Increments?

The two steps of the Method of Increments are first, find a formula for $\Delta d/\Delta t$, and second, take the limit of $\Delta d/\Delta t$ as Δt approaches 0.

7. In a single sentence, what is the general procedure for finding instantaneous speed?

The general procedure for finding instantaneous speed is to find a formula for $\Delta d/\Delta t$ where Δt is no longer in the denominator, then substitute 0 for Δt.

8. Using the Method of Increments, find the instantaneous speed of a falling object after it has fallen 2 seconds. Approach the instant from times less than 2 seconds. Compare with your answer from question 5.

$$
\begin{aligned}
\frac{\Delta d}{\Delta t} &= \frac{d(2)-d(2-\Delta t)}{\Delta t} = \frac{16(2)^2-16(2-\Delta t)^2}{\Delta t} = \frac{64-16(2-\Delta t)(2-\Delta t)}{\Delta t} = \\
&= \frac{64-16(4-4\Delta t+(\Delta t)^2)}{\Delta t} = \frac{64-64+64\Delta t-16(\Delta t)^2}{\Delta t} = \frac{64\Delta t-16(\Delta t)^2}{\Delta t} \\
&= 64-16\Delta t \qquad (\Delta t \neq 0) \\
v_2 &= \lim_{\Delta t \to 0}(64-16\Delta t) = 64 \text{ ft/s}
\end{aligned}
$$

9. Why ought we to be amazed at our ability to arrive at a method for calculating instantaneous speed? How is this related to the Platonic-Pythagorean view of the world?

We ought to be amazed at our ability to arrive at a method for calculating instantaneous speed because we arrived at a relation between instantaneous speed and time *without doing any experiments whatsoever.* This is an affirmation of the Platonic-Pythagorean view of the world that the world can be descrived mathematically because we discovered something true about the world using just mathematics.

10. What are the three central concepts of calculus? What mathematical law ties them all together? Which have we studied so far?

The three central concepts of calculus are: the limit of a function, the derivative of a function, and the integral of a function. The Fundamental Theorem of Calculus ties them all together. So far we have studied the limit of a function.

11. The free fall formula for objects near the surface of Jupiter is roughly

$$d(t) = 40t^2$$

Using the Method of Increments, find the velocity function for objects near Jupiter's surface. Approach the instant t from times less than t.

$$\frac{\Delta d}{\Delta t} = \frac{d(t) - d(t-\Delta t)}{\Delta t} = \frac{40(t)^2 - 40(t-\Delta t)^2}{\Delta t} = \frac{40t^2 - 40(t-\Delta t)(t-\Delta t)}{\Delta t}$$

$$= \frac{40t^2 - 40(t^2 - 2t\Delta t + (\Delta t)^2)}{\Delta t} = \frac{40t^2 - 40t^2 + 80t\Delta t - 40(\Delta t)^2}{\Delta t}$$

$$= \frac{80t\Delta t - 40(\Delta t)^2}{\Delta t} = 80t - 40\Delta t$$

$$v(t) = \lim_{\Delta t \to 0}(80t - 40\Delta t) = 80t$$

12. Express, "The instantaneous rate of change in y with respect to x" using symbols.

$$\lim_{\Delta x \to 0}\left(\frac{\Delta y}{\Delta x}\right)$$

13. Express, "The average rate of change in y with respect to x" using symbols.

$$\frac{\Delta y}{\Delta x}$$

14. Are all derivatives limits? Are all limits derivatives?
All derivatives are limits, but not all limits are derivatives.

15. For $y(x)$=$5x^2$, find the limit of $y(x)$ as x approaches 3.

$$\lim_{x\to 3} y(x) = \lim_{x\to 3} 5x^2 = 5(3)^2 = 5\cdot 9 = 45$$

16. Using the Method of Increments, find the function for the instantaneous rate of change for $f(x) = 2x^3$.

$f(x) = 2x^3$

$\leftarrow \Delta x \rightarrow$

$x_1 = x$ $\quad$ $x_2 = x + \Delta x$

$y_1 = 2x^3$ $\quad$ $y_2 = 2(x+\Delta x)^3$

$$\frac{\Delta y}{\Delta x} = \frac{y(x+\Delta x) - y(x)}{\Delta x} = \frac{2(x+\Delta x)^3 - 2(x)^3}{\Delta x} = \frac{2(x+\Delta x)(x+\Delta x)(x+\Delta x) - 2x^3}{\Delta x}$$

$$= \frac{2(x^3 + 2x\Delta x + x(\Delta x)^2(x+\Delta x) - 2x^3}{\Delta x} =$$

$$= \frac{2(x^3 + 2x^2\Delta x + x(\Delta x)^2 + x^2\Delta x + 2x(\Delta x)^2 + (\Delta x)^3) - 2x^3}{\Delta x} =$$

$$= \frac{\cancel{2x^3} + \cancel{4x^2\Delta x}\ \cancel{2x(\Delta x)^2} + \cancel{2x^2\Delta x} + \cancel{4x(\Delta x)^2} + 2(\Delta x)^3 - \cancel{2x^3}}{\Delta x} =$$

$$= \frac{6x^2\Delta x + 6x(\Delta x)^2 + 2(\Delta x)^3}{\Delta x} = 6x^2 + 6x\Delta x + 2(\Delta x)^2$$

$f'(x)$ is the function that gives the instantaneous rate of change for $f(x) = 2x^3$, and so $f'(x) = \lim_{\Delta x\to 0}(6x^2 + 6x\Delta x + 2(\Delta x)^2) = 6x^2$.

17. Why is bx called a "first-order" term?

bx is called a first-order term because its highest degree is 1, that is, the highest exponent is 1. We could rewrite bx as bx^1.

18. How might you write $y(x) = c$ as a function of x?

$y(x) = c$ can be written as a function of x in this way: $y(x) = cx^0$. We remember that anything to the power of 0 is 1 and since anything multiplied by 1 is itself, we have two functions stated differently that mean the same thing—one with the x and one without.

19. In terms of our prime notation, how would you denote the derivative of $y(x) = f(x) + g(x) + u(x)$?

In terms of our prime notation, the derivative of $y(x) = f(x) + g(x) + u(x)$ would be $y'(x) = f'(x) + g'(x) + u'(x)$.

20. Using the Method of Increments, and approaching the value we're interested in, x, from values greater than x, find the derivative of $y(x) = bx$.

$$y(x) = bx$$

$$\frac{\Delta y}{\Delta x} = \frac{y(x+\Delta x)-y(x)}{\Delta x} = \frac{b(x+\Delta x)-bx}{\Delta x} = \frac{bx+b\Delta x-bx}{\Delta x} = \frac{b\Delta x}{\Delta x} = b$$

$$(\Delta x \neq 0)$$

$$\frac{dy}{dx} = \lim_{\Delta x \to 0}\left[\frac{\Delta y}{\Delta x}\right] = \lim_{\Delta x \to 0}(b) = b = \frac{dy}{dx}$$

21. Using the Power Rule, find the derivatives for the following power functions:

a. $y(x) = 4x^3$

Answer:

$$y(x) = 4x^3 \quad \Rightarrow \quad y' = 3 \cdot 4x^{3-1} = 12x^2$$

b. $V(r) = \frac{4}{3}\pi r^3$

Answer:

$$V(r) = \frac{4}{3}\pi r^3 \quad \Rightarrow \quad \frac{dV}{dr} = 3\left[\frac{4}{3}\right]\pi r^{3-1} \quad = 4\pi r^2$$

c. $y(x) = -16x^{-2} + 5x$

Answer:

$$y(x) = -16x^{-2} + 5x \quad \Rightarrow \quad y'(x) = -2\cdot(-16)x^{-2-1} + 1\cdot 5x^{1-1} =$$
$$= 32x^{-3} + 5 \quad = \frac{32}{x^3} + 5$$

d. $y(x) = 2x^{100}$

Answer:

$$y(x) = 2x^{100} \quad \Rightarrow \quad \frac{dy}{dx} = 100\cdot 2x^{100-1} \quad = 200x^{99}$$

e. $z(x) = \frac{1}{x}$

Answer:

$$z(x) = \frac{1}{x} = x^{-1} \quad \Rightarrow \quad z'(x) = -1\cdot x^{-1-1} \quad = -x^{-2} \quad = -\frac{1}{x^2}$$

f. $y(x) = \frac{1}{x} + 4x^{16} + 9x^9 + 1$

Answer:

$$y(x) = \frac{1}{x} + 4x^{16} + 9x^9 + 1 \quad = \quad -x^{-1} + 4x^{16} + 9x^9 + x^0$$
$$\Rightarrow \quad y'(x) = -1\cdot x^{-1-1} + 16\cdot 4x^{16-1} + 9\cdot 9x^{9-1} + 0\cdot x^{0-1} =$$
$$= -x^{-2} + 64x^{15} + 81x^8 = -\frac{1}{x^2} + 64x^{15} + 81x^8$$

CALCULUS FOR EVERYONE

EXAM 3: ANSWER KEY

CHAPTERS 15-20

1. Why are the units of acceleration ft/s^2 or m/s^2? In other words, why the odd phrase "second *squared*"?

   The units of acceleration are ft/s^2 or m/s^2. The real meaning of these units comes through when we say them in word—"feet per second per second." Feet per second is the unit for velocity, and the other "per second" tells us that the velocity is changing every second.

2. Why did we add the negative sign to Galileo's law of fall?

   We added the negative sign to Galileo's law of fall to show that a dropped object is moving downwards.

3. What does it mean to "interpret" mathematics?

   Numbers, by themselves, don't tell us much of anything. They need to be interpreted to have meaning. To understand what numbers are saying about the world we need to know the numbers, what they represent, and the context in which they are operating. For example, we wouldn't know what $d(t) = 16t^2$ means except that we were told the context for this function (it describes a situation in which an object is dropped near the earth and air resistance can be ignored). We were told that t represents the amount of time that has elapsed since the moment the object was dropped, and d represents the distance the object has fallen in that time. Once we had all this information, we could interpret the function and its output.

4. Who revived the Platonic-Pythagorean tradition during the Scientific Revolution?

   Galileo revived the Platonic-Pythagorrean tradition during the Scientific Revolution.

5. What are the two main theories of contemporary physics?

   The two main theories of contemporary physics are general relativity and quantum mechanics.

6. Suppose that a golf ball is launched straight up in the air, and its height above the ground is given by the following function:

$$h(t) = -16t^2 + 200t + 6$$

a. What are the functions that describe the ball's velocity and acceleration?

$$v(t) = h'(t) = -32t + 200$$
$$a(t) = v'(t) = h''(t) = -32$$

b. At what height above the ground does the ball's travel begin? What is the ball's speed at that time?

$$h(0) = -16(0)^2 + 200(0) + 6 = 6 \text{ ft}$$
$$v(0) = -32(0) + 200 = 200 \text{ ft/s}$$

c. When is the ball at its highest? What is the maximum height?

$$v = 0 = -32t + 200 \quad \Rightarrow \quad 32t = 200 \quad \Rightarrow \quad t = \frac{200}{32} = \frac{100}{16} = \frac{25}{4} = 6.25 \text{ s}$$

$$\begin{aligned} h(6.25) &= -16(6.25)^2 + 200(6.25) + 6 \\ &= -625 + 1250 + 6 \\ &= 631 \text{ ft} \end{aligned}$$

7. Find the velocity and acceleration functions for the general free fall formula for objects near the earth's surface.

$$h(t) = -16t^2 + v_0t + h_0$$

Answer:

$$h(t) = -16t^2 + v_{.0}t + h_0$$
$$v(t) = -32t + v_0$$
$$a(t) = -32$$

8. Geometrically, what is the derivative of a function?

Geometrically, the derivative of a function is the slope of that function.

9. Why do we talk about the slope*s* (plural) of a parabola?

We talk about the slopes (plural) of a parabola because a parabola curves and so its steepness is constantly changing. This means that a parabola has a different slope at any given point, and so it has many different slopes.

10. Why doesn't it make sense to talk about secant lines and tangent lines of a *straight line*?

It doesn't make sense to talk about secant lines and tangent lines of a straight line because there are no secant or tangent lines of a straight line. There are no secant lines of a straight line because no line can cut the straight line at just two points, and there are no tangent lines because there are no lines that can touch only a single point on the straight line and still have the same slope.

11. In terms of the delta notation, what is the slope of the secant line?

In terms of delta notation, the slope of the secant line is $\frac{\Delta y}{\Delta x}$.

12. Write out the symbolic definition of a derivative and label it in terms of the slope of a secant line and the slope of a tangent line.

The symbolic definition of a derivative is $y' = \frac{dy}{dx} = \lim_{\Delta x \to 0}\left(\frac{\Delta y}{\Delta x}\right)$

$\frac{dy}{dx}$ **refers to the slope of the tangent line.**

$\lim_{\Delta x \to 0}\left(\frac{\Delta y}{\Delta x}\right)$ **refers to the slope of the secant line as** Δx **approaches 0.**

13. In symbols, what is the *average* slope?

In symbols, the average slope is $\frac{\Delta y}{\Delta x}$.

14. In symbols, what is the *instantaneous* slope? What does instantaneous mean if we're not talking about time?

In symbols, the instantaneous slope is $\frac{dy}{dx}$.

"Instantaneous" does not necessarily indicate an instant in time but the instantaneous rate of change of y **with respect to x.**

15. Using the Method of Increments, find the *function* that can give the slope of $y(x) = x^2$ at any x-value. Approach x from values *less than* x. Then find the slope of $y(x)$ at $x = 1$, $x = -1$, and at $x = 5$. Draw the relevant information on a Cartesian coordinate system.

$$y(x) = x^2$$

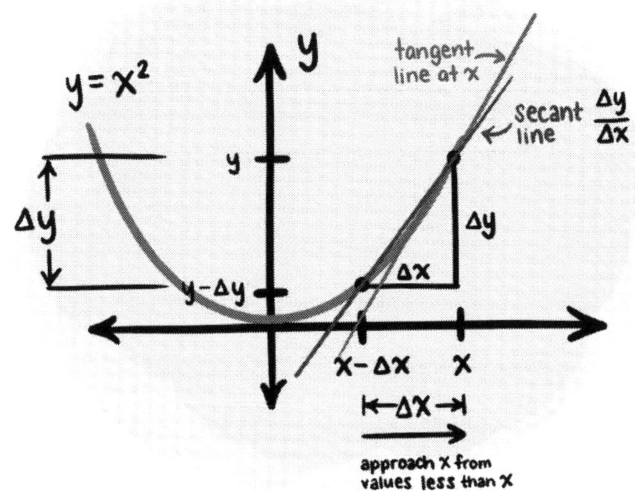

$$\frac{\Delta y}{\Delta x} = \frac{y(x) - y(x - \Delta x)}{\Delta x}$$

$$= \frac{x^2 - (x - \Delta x)^2}{\Delta x}$$

$$= \frac{x^2 - (x - \Delta x)(x - \Delta x)}{\Delta x}$$

$$= \frac{x^2 - (x^2 - 2x\Delta x + (\Delta x)^2)}{\Delta x}$$

$$= \frac{x^2 - x^2 + 2x\Delta x - (\Delta x)^2}{\Delta x} = \frac{2x\Delta x - (\Delta x)^2}{\Delta x} = 2x - \Delta x \qquad (\Delta x \neq 0)$$

$$\text{Slope} = y'(x)\ \frac{dy}{dx} = \lim_{\Delta x \to 0}(2x - \Delta x) = 2x$$

$$\left.\frac{dy}{dx}\right|_{x=1} = y'(2) = 2(1) = 2$$

$$\left.\frac{dy}{dx}\right|_{x=-1} = y'(-1) = 2(-1) = -2$$

$$\left.\frac{dy}{dx}\right|_{x=5} = y'(5) = 2(5) = 10$$

16. Using the Power Rule, find the *function* that can give the slope of $y(t) = -16t^2$ at any t-value. Then find the slope of $y(t)$ at $t = 0$, $t = 2$, and at $t = 8$.

$$y(t) = -16t^2 \qquad \frac{dy}{dt} = 2\cdot(-16)t^{2-1} = -32t = y'(t)$$

$$\left.\frac{dy}{dt}\right|_{t=0} = -32(0) = 0$$

$$\left.\frac{dy}{dt}\right|_{t=2} = -32(2) = -64$$

$$\left.\frac{dy}{dt}\right|_{t=8} = -32(8) = -256$$

17. From memory, draw and label the *physical* picture of an object whose motion is described by Galileo's law of fall, $d(t) = 16t^2$. Use a straightedge.

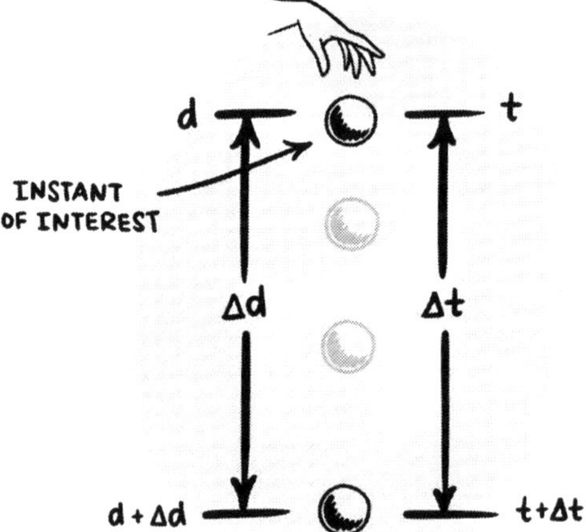

18. From memory, draw and label the *mathematical* picture of an object who's motion is described by Galileo's law of fall, $d(t) = 16t^2$. Use a straightedge. Make sure to draw the line that represents the average speed between t and $t + \Delta t$, and the line representing the instantaneous speed at t.

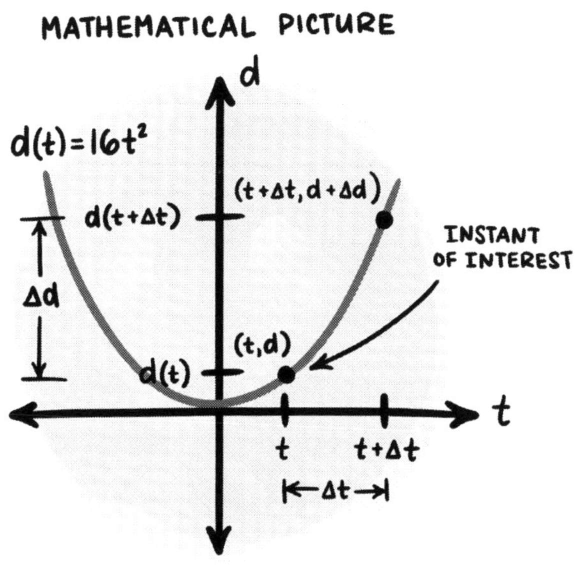

19. Consider the following graph of $y(x)$'s derivative:

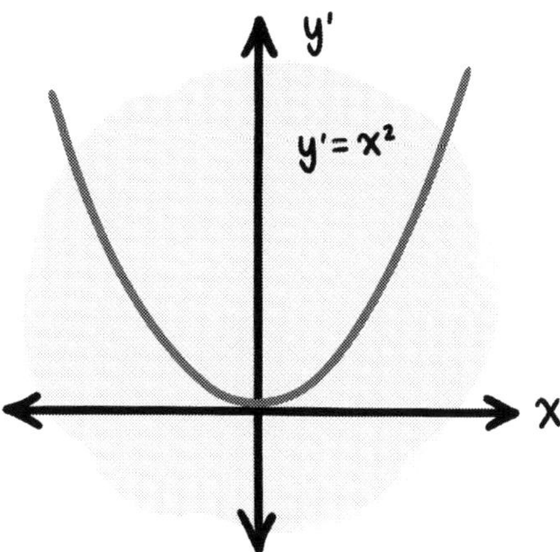

a. From just this graph, what do you know about the slope of the original function $y(x)$ for values of $x < 0$, $x = 0$, and $x > 0$?

Since the *values* of $y' = x^2$ are positive for $x < 0$, the *slope* of y (the original function) is positive for values of $x < 0$, that is, y slopes upward (when moving from left to right).

Since the *value* of $y' = x^2$ is 0 when $x = 0$, the *slope* of y (the original function) is 0 at $x = 0$, that is, y is flat exactly at $x = 0$.

Since the *values* of $y' = x^2$ are positive for $x > 0$, the *slope* of y (the original function) is positive for values of $x > 0$, that is, y slopes upward (when moving from left to right).

b. From just this graph, does the slope of the original function $y(x)$ get steeper, flatter, or stay constant for x-values greater than 0 as x moves away from 0?

As x-values move away from 0 to the right, the values of the derivative $y' = x^2$ increase, meaning that the slope of $y(x)$ gets steeper.

c. From just this graph, does the slope of the original function $y(x)$ get steeper, flatter, or stay constant for x-values less than 0 as x approaches 0?

As x-values approach 0 from the left, the values of the derivative $y' = x^2$ decrease, meaning that the slope of $y(x)$ gets less steep or flatter.

20. For the graph of Galileo's free fall, what happens at $t < 0$?

For the graph of Galileo's free fall, any time less than 0 is meaningless. The graph does not tell us anything about what happens before an object is dropped at $t = 0$.

21. Consider the following free fall graph (the height, velocity, and acceleration functions cross the vertical axis at 80 ft, -30 ft/s, and -32 ft/s^2, respectively):

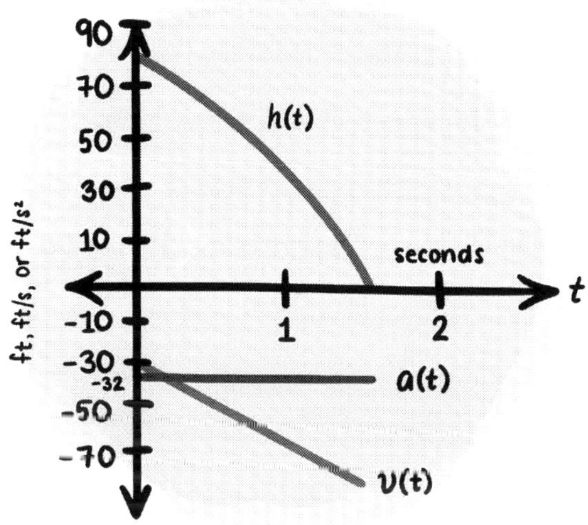

a. What is the slope of $h(t)$ at $t = 0$?

To find the slope of $h(t)$ we can look at $v(t)$. The value of $v(t)$ at $t = 0$ is –30. That is, $v(0) = –30$. Therefore, the slope of $h(t)$ at $t = 0$ is –30 or –30/1.

b. What is the slope of $v(t)$?

The slope of $v(t)$ is the same everywhere (that is, it's constant) and is given by the values of $a(t)$, which is –32 or –32/1.

c. What are the formulas for $h(t)$, $v(t)$, and $a(t)$?

We know that the general form of $h(t)$ is

$$h(t) = -16t^2 + v_0 t + h_0$$

From the graph we see that h_0 = 80 ft and v_0 = –30 ft/s and so

$$h(t) = -16t^2 - 30t + 80$$

So then

$$v(t) = h't = -32t - 30$$

and

$$a(t) = h''t = v'(t) = -32$$

as always.

CALCULUS FOR EVERYONE

EXAM 4: ANSWER KEY

COMPREHENSIVE FINAL EXAM

---

1. Where did we get the original Power Rule?

   We got the original Power Rule by using the Method of Increments.

2. Using the Reverse Power Rule, find the anti-derivatives of the following power functions. (You can always check your work by taking the derivative of your answer.)

   a. $y'(x) = 6x^3$

   Answer:

   $$y'(x) = 6x^3$$

   $$y(x) = \frac{6}{3+1}x^{3+1} + C = \frac{6}{4}x^4 + C = \frac{3}{2}x^4 + C$$

   b. $z(x) = \frac{1}{x}$

   Answer:

   $z(x) = \frac{1}{x} = x^{-1}$ We can't use the Reverse Power Rule for $n = -1$.

c. $f(x) = 9x^7 - \pi\sqrt[3]{x} + \frac{1}{\sqrt{x}} + x$

Answer:

$$f(x) = 9x^7 - \pi\sqrt[3]{x} + \frac{1}{\sqrt{x}} + x = 9x^7 - \pi x^{\frac{1}{3}} + x^{-\frac{1}{2}} + x$$

$$F(x) = \left[\frac{9}{7+1}x^{7+1} + C_1\right] - \left[\frac{\pi}{\frac{1}{3}+\frac{3}{3}}x^{\frac{1}{3}+\frac{3}{3}} + C_2\right] + \left[\frac{1}{-\frac{1}{2}+\frac{2}{2}}x^{-\frac{1}{2}+\frac{2}{2}} + C_3\right] +$$

$$+\left[\frac{1}{1+1}x^{1+1} + C_4\right] =$$

NOTE: The negative sign in front of the second parentheses gets distributed, but a constant minus a constant is still a constant.

$$= \frac{9}{8}x^8 - \frac{\pi}{\frac{4}{3}}x^{\frac{4}{3}} + \frac{1}{\frac{3}{2}}x^{\frac{3}{2}} + \frac{1}{\frac{1}{2}}x^{\frac{1}{2}} + C =$$

$$F(x) = \frac{9}{8}x^8 - \frac{3\pi}{4}x^{\frac{4}{3}} + \frac{2}{3}x^{\frac{3}{2}} + 2\sqrt{x} + C$$

3. What is the derivative of

$f(x) = \frac{a}{n+1}x^{n+1} + C$

Answer:

$$f(x) = \frac{a}{n+1}x^{n+1} + C \qquad = \frac{a}{n+1}x^{n+1} + Cx^0$$

$$f'(x) = (n+1)\frac{a}{(n+1)}x^{(n+1)-1} + 0 \cdot C\,x^{0-1} =$$

$$f'(x) = a\,x^n$$

4. Using the Reverse Power Rule, find the height, velocity, and acceleration functions for the following situations:

a. An object dropped from a height of 100 feet.

We begin with $a(t) = -32$ for any freefall case. To find $v(t)$ we note that $v(0) = 0$ because the object was dropped.

$$v(t) = A(t) = \frac{-32}{0+1}t^{0+1} + C = -32t + C$$
$$v_0 = v(0) = 0 = -32(0) + C \quad \Rightarrow \quad C = 0$$

Therefore,

$$v(t) = -32t$$

Now, we know that $h(0) = 100$, and so

$$h(t) = v(t) = \frac{-32}{1+1}t^{1+1} + C = \frac{-32}{2}t^2 + C = -16t^2 + C$$
$$h(0) = 100 = -16(0)^2 + C \quad \Rightarrow \quad C = 100$$

Therefore,

$$h(t) = -16t^2 + 100$$

b. An object thrown straight up in the air at a speed of 25 ft/s from a height of 50 ft.

$a(t) = -32$, which is the same for all free fall cases.

$$v(t) = \frac{-32}{0+1}t^{0\ 1} + C = -32t + C$$
$$v(0) = 25 = -32(0) + C \quad \Rightarrow \quad C = 25$$

Therefore,

$$v(t) = -32t + 25$$

$$h(t) = V(t) = \frac{-32}{1+1}t^{1+1} + C_1 + \frac{25t}{0+1}t^{0+1} + C_2 = -16t^2 + 25t + C$$
$$h(0) = 50 = -16(0)^2 + 25(0) + C \quad \Rightarrow \quad C = 50$$

Therefore,

$$h(t) = -16t^2 + 25t + 50$$

c. An object in free fall whose behavior is described by the following graph:

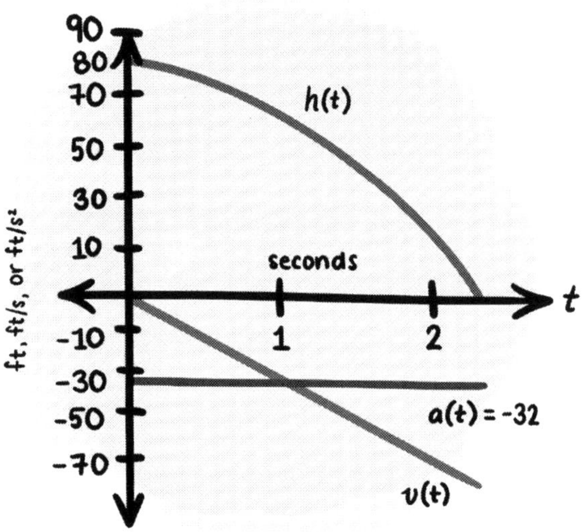

As usual $a(t) = -32$

$$v(t) = A(t) = \frac{-32}{0+1}t^{0+1} + C_1 = -32t + C_1$$

From the graph we see that at $t = 0$, $v(t) = 0$ and so

$$v(0) = 0 = -32(0) + C_1 \quad \Rightarrow \quad C_1 = 0$$

Therefore,

$$v(t) = -32t$$

$$h(t) = \frac{-32}{1+1}t^{1+1} + C_2 = -16t^2 + C_2$$

From the graph we see that at $t = 0$, $h(t) = 80$ and so

$$h(0) = 80 = -16(0)^2 + C_2 \quad \Rightarrow \quad C_2 = 80$$

Therefore,

$$h(t) = -16t^2 + 80$$

d. An object in free fall whose behavior is described by the following graph:

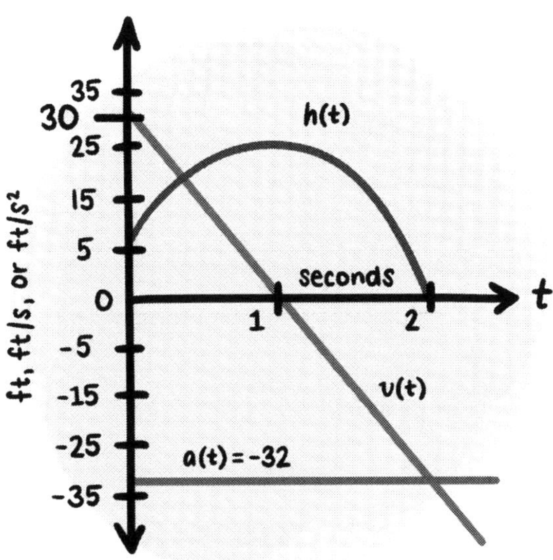

$a(t) = -32$

$$v(t) = A(t) = \frac{-32}{0+1}t^{0+1} + C_1 = -32t + C_1$$

From the graph we see that at $t = 0$, $v(t) = 30$ and so

$$v(0) = 30 = -32(0) + C_1 \quad \Rightarrow \quad C_1 = 30$$

Therefore,

$$v(t) = -32t + 30$$

$$h(t) = V(t) = \frac{-32}{1+1}t^{1+1}C_2 + \frac{30}{0+1}t^{0+1} + C_3$$

$$= -16t^2 + 30t + C$$

From the graph we see that at $t = 0$, $h(t) = 5$ and so

$$h(0) = 5 = -16(0)^2 + 30(0) + C \quad \Rightarrow \quad C = 5$$

Therefore,

$$h(t) = -16t^2 + 30t + 5$$

5. What do we call the case of overestimating? Of underestimating?

   In the case of overestimating, we say "circumscribed," and in the case of underestimating, we say "inscribed."

6. In terms of S_n, and the limit of notation, give the definition of the integral.

   In terms of S_n, and the limit of notation, the definition of the integral is $A = \lim_{n\to\infty} S_n$.

7. In terms of A_i's and the limit notation, give the definition of the integral.

   In terms of A_i's and the limit notation, the definition of the integral is $A = \lim_{n\to\infty}\left[A_1 + A_2 + A_3 + A_4 + \cdots + A_n\right]$.

8. In terms of y's and Δx's and the limit notation, give the definition of the integral.

   In terms of y's and Δx's and the limit notation, the definition of the integral is $A = \lim_{n\to\infty}\left[(y_1\cdot\Delta x)+(y_2\cdot\Delta x)+(y_3\cdot\Delta x)+(y_4\cdot\Delta x)+\cdots+(y_n\cdot\Delta x)\right.$

9. What is

   $$\lim_{n\to\infty} S_n$$

   in terms of our elongated "s" integral notation? What does "*ydx*" as a whole stand for? What does *y* stand for? What does *dx* stand for?

   In terms of our elongated "s" integral notation, $\lim_{x\to\infty} S_n$ *is* $\int_a^b ydx$. **As a whole, "*ydx*" stands for the area of each infinitely thin mini-rectangle. *y* stands for the height of each mini-rectangle, and *dx* stands for the base of each mini-rectangle.**

10. What do a and b stand for in the following formula?

$$\int_a^b y\,dx$$

In the formula $\int_a^b y\,dx$, the a and b stand for the x-values of the endpoints of the entire area's base.

11. What does "$f(x)dx$" as a whole stand for in the following formula?

$$\int_a^b f(x)\,dx$$

What does $f(x)$ stand for? What does dx stand for?

As a whole, "$f(x)dx$" stands for the area of each infinitely thin mini-rectangle. $f(x)$ stands for the height of each mini-rectangle, and dx stands for the base of each mini-rectangle.

12. Find

$$\int_0^5 x^2\,dx$$

beginning with an *overestimation* of the sum of the mini-rectangles.

Integral of $y = x^2$ from $x = 0$ to $x = 5$.

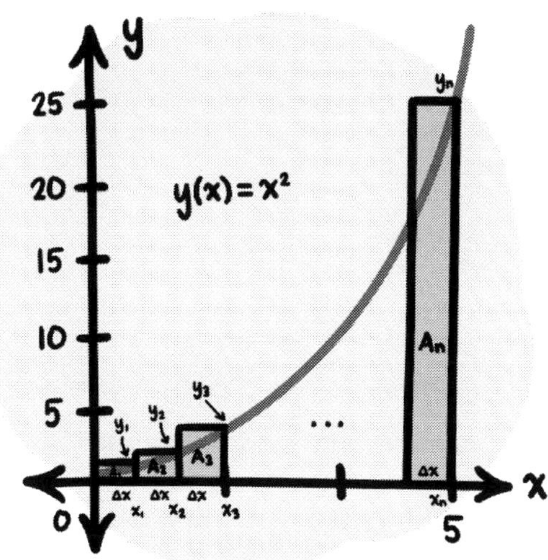

i	x_i	y_i
1	$x_1 = \Delta x$	$y_1 = (\Delta x)^2$
2	$x_2 = 2\Delta x$	$y_2 = (2\Delta x)^2 = 4(\Delta x)^2$
3	$x_3 = 3\Delta x$	$y_3 = (3\Delta x)^2 = 9(\Delta x)^2$
$\vdots$	$\vdots$	$\vdots$
n	$x_n = n\Delta x$	$y_n = (n\Delta x)^2 = n^2(\Delta x)^2$

$$\overline{S}_n = (\Delta x)^2 \Delta x + 4(\Delta x)^2 \Delta x + 9(\Delta x)^2 \Delta x + \cdots + n^2(\Delta x)^2 \Delta x =$$

$$= (\Delta x)^3 + 4(\Delta x)^3 + 9(\Delta x)^3 + \cdots + n^2(\Delta x)^3 =$$

$$= (\Delta x)^3 \underbrace{\left[1^2 + 2^2 + 3^2 + \cdots + n^2\right]}_{\frac{n^3}{3}+\frac{n^2}{2}+\frac{n}{6}} =$$

$$= (\Delta x)^3 \left[\frac{n^3}{3} + \frac{n^2}{2} + \frac{n}{6}\right]$$

We need Δx in terms of n:

$$\Delta x = \frac{5-0}{n} = \frac{5}{n}$$

$$\underline{S}_n = \left[\frac{5}{n}\right]^3 \left[\frac{n^3}{3} + \frac{n^2}{2} + \frac{n}{6}\right] = \frac{125}{n^3}\left[\frac{n^3}{3} + \frac{n^2}{2} + \frac{n}{6}\right] =$$

$$= 125\left[\frac{1}{3} + \frac{1}{2n} + \frac{1}{6n^2}\right] = \frac{125}{3} + \frac{125}{2n} + \frac{125}{6n^2}$$

$$\Rightarrow \quad A = \int_0^5 x^2 dx = \lim_{n\to\infty}\left[\frac{125}{3} + \frac{125}{2n} + \frac{125}{6n^2}\right] = \frac{125}{3}$$

13. What are the three central concepts in calculus? What ties them all together?

The three central concepts in calculus are the limit, derivative, and integral of a function. The Fundamental Theorem of Calculus ties them all together.

14. In terms of limits, what is the formula for the definition of a derivative?

The formula for the definition of a derivative is $\frac{dy}{dx} = \lim_{\Delta x \to 0}\left(\frac{\Delta y}{\Delta x}\right)$.

15. In terms of limits, what is the formula for the definition of an integral?

The formula for the definition of an integral is $\int_a^b y(x)dx = \lim_{n \to \infty} S_n$.

16. Calculuate the following definite integral:

$\int_1^3 6x^3dx$

Answer:

$$\int_1^3 6x^3dx = \frac{6}{4}x^4 + C\Big|_1^3 = \left[\frac{3}{2}(3)^4 + C\right] - \left[\frac{3}{2}(1)^4 + C\right] =$$

$$= \frac{3(81)}{2} + C - \frac{3}{2} - C = \frac{243}{2} - \frac{3}{2} = \frac{240}{2} = 120$$

17. Find the following indefinite integrals:

a. $\int x^2dx$

Answer:

$$\int x^2dx = \frac{1}{3}x^3 + C$$

b. $\int\left(-\frac{3\sqrt{x}}{7}\right)dx$

Answer:

$$\int\left[-\frac{3\sqrt{x}}{7}\right]dx = \int\left[-\frac{3}{7}x^{\frac{1}{2}}\right]dx = -\frac{3}{7}\cdot\frac{1}{\left[\frac{1}{2}+\frac{2}{2}\right]}x^{\frac{1}{2}+\frac{2}{3}} + C =$$

$$= -\frac{3}{7\cdot\frac{3}{2}}x^{\frac{3}{2}} + C = -\frac{2}{7}x^{\frac{3}{2}} + C = -\frac{2}{7}\sqrt{x^3} + C$$

18. Using the Fundamental Theorem of Calculus, find the height, velocity, and acceleration functions for an object dropped from a height of 100 feet.

We know that for *any* free fall scenario that $a(t) = -32$ and that
$v(t) = A(t) = \int(-32)dt = -32t + C.$
In *this* particular case, we're told that $v(0) = 0$ (because the object is simply dropped) and so

$$v_0 = v(0) = 0 = -32(0) + C \quad \Rightarrow \quad C = 0$$

This gives us

$$v(t) = -32t.$$

Now,

$$h(t) = v(t) = \int -32t dt = -\frac{32}{2}t^2 + C = -16t^2 + C,$$

where,

$$h(0) = 100 = -16(0)^2 + C \quad \Rightarrow \quad C = 100$$

and so

$$h(t) = -16t^2 + 100.$$

19. What geometrical property is the derivative associated with? What physical quantities can this geometrical property be associated with?

Geometrically, the derivative is associated with the slope of a function. This geometrical property, slope, can be associated with the physical properties of speed and acceleration.

20. What geometrical property is the integral associated with? What physical quantities can this geometrical property be associated with? Why didn't we talk about this earlier when introducing integrals?

Geometrically, the integral is associated with areas, specifically, the areas under a function's curve. This geometrical property, area, can be associated with the physical properties of "change in velocity" and "change in height." We didn't talk about the physical association of

this geometrical property earlier because we didn't have a relatively simple method to calculate integrals, not until we explored the Fundamental Theorem of Calculus.

21. What physical property is represented by the area "under" the acceleration curve?

The physical property represented by the area "under" the acceleration curve is "change in velocity."

22. What physical property is represented by the area "under" the velocity curve?

The physical property represented by the area "under" the velocity curve is "change in distance" or "change in height" in the case of free fall.

23. Find the change in height and velocity between *a* seconds and *b* seconds for a free fall situation described by the following formula:

$$h(t) = -16t^2 + v_0 t + h_0$$

This exercise is asking you to make a very general calculation, one that represents any beginning time and any ending time. As usual,

$$h(t) = -16t^2 + v_0 t + h_0 \quad \Rightarrow \quad v(t) = -32t + v_0 \quad \Rightarrow \quad a(t) = -32$$

The change in speed, Δv, is given by the area "under" the acceleration curve (let's again call it A_a, where the subscript *a* stands for "acceleration" and not for the beginning of time, which we also called *a*).

$$\Delta v = A_a = \int_a^b -32\,dt = -32t\Big| + C_a^b = -32(b) + C - \left[-32(a) + C\right] =$$
$$= -32 \cdot b + 32 \cdot a = -32(b - a)$$

The change in the height, Δh, is given by the area "under" the velocity curve (let's call is A_v):

$$\Delta h = A_v = \int_a^b (-32t + v_0)\,dt = -16t^2 + v_0 t + C\Big|_a^b =$$
$$= -16(b)^2 + v_0(b) + C - \left[-16(a)^2 + v_0(a) + C\right] =$$
$$= -16b^2 + v_0 b + 16a^2 - v_0 a =$$
$$= -16(b^2 - a^2) + v_0(b - a)$$

24. What were the three Pythagorean ideas that were at the foundation of the Scientific Revolution?

The three Pythagorean ideas that were at the foundation of the Scientific Revolution were that the universe is ordered according to perfect mathematical laws, that divine reason is the orderer, and that human reason can discern the divine mathematical pattern.

25. Using calculus, solve Zeno's paradox.

Zeno's paradox can be mathematically formulated by noting that the progressive dividing in half of the total distance (say, one mile) can be written as follows:

$$\text{Sum} = \frac{1}{2} + \frac{1}{4} + \frac{1}{8} + \frac{1}{16} + \cdots$$

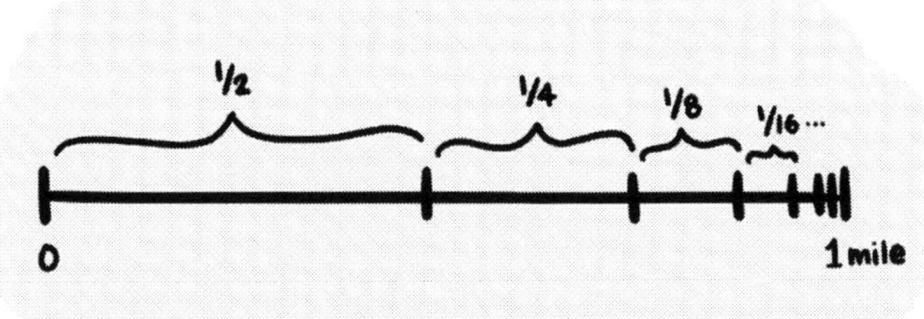

We can write the above sum in terms of *n* number of divisions (let's call this definite sum, Sum_n):

$$\text{Sum}_n = \frac{1}{2} + \frac{1}{4} + \frac{1}{8} + \frac{1}{16} + \cdots + \frac{1}{2^n} =$$
$$= \frac{1}{2^1} + \frac{1}{2^2} + \frac{1}{2^3} + \frac{1}{2^4} + \cdots + \frac{1}{2^n}$$

To get rid of the "..." we note the simple and obvious fact (though it's not obvious at first *why* we would do this) that

$$\text{Sum}_n = \frac{1}{2}\text{Sum}_n + \frac{1}{2}\text{Sum}_n .$$

This can be rearranged as follows (though again, it might not seem to be entirely clear at this stage why we would do this):

$$\text{Sum}_n - \frac{1}{2}\text{Sum}_n = \frac{1}{2}\text{Sum}_n .$$

Let's now write this subtraction problem vertically:

$$\begin{array}{l} \text{Sum}_n \\ -\frac{1}{2}\text{Sum}_n \\ \hline \frac{1}{2}\text{Sum}_n \end{array}$$

And $\frac{1}{2}\text{Sum}_n$ is equal to

$$\begin{aligned} \frac{1}{2}\text{Sum}_n &= \frac{1}{2}\cdot\left[\frac{1}{2^1}+\frac{1}{2^2}+\frac{1}{2^3}+\frac{1}{2^4}+\cdots+\frac{1}{2^n}\right] \\ &= \frac{1}{2^1\cdot 2^1}+\frac{1}{2^1\cdot 2^2}+\frac{1}{2^1\cdot 2^3}+\frac{1}{2^1\cdot 2^4}+\cdots+\frac{1}{2^1\cdot 2^n} \\ &= \frac{1}{2^{1+1}}+\frac{1}{2^{2+1}}+\frac{1}{2^{3+1}}+\frac{1}{2^{4+1}}+\cdots+\frac{1}{2^{n+1}} \\ &= \frac{1}{2^2}+\frac{1}{2^3}+\frac{1}{2^4}+\frac{1}{2^5}+\cdots+\frac{1}{2^{n+1}} \end{aligned}$$

Plugging this result into the vertical subtraction problem:

$$\begin{array}{rl} \text{Sum}_n &= \frac{1}{2^1}+\cancel{\frac{1}{2^2}}+\cancel{\frac{1}{2^3}}+\cancel{\frac{1}{2^4}}+\cancel{\frac{1}{2^5}}+\cdots+\cancel{\frac{1}{2^n}} \\ -\frac{1}{2}\text{Sum}_n &= \cancel{\frac{1}{2^2}}+\cancel{\frac{1}{2^3}}+\cancel{\frac{1}{2^4}}+\cancel{\frac{1}{2^5}}+\cdots\cancel{\frac{1}{2^n}}+\frac{1}{2^{n+1}} \\ \hline \frac{1}{2}\text{Sum}_n &= \frac{1}{2}-\frac{1}{2^{n+1}} \end{array}$$

Taking this answer to the subtraction problem, solve for Sum_n (the algebra is carried out in a slightly different order than in the chapter but it's entirely equivalent):

$$\begin{aligned}\text{Sum}_n &= 2\left[\frac{1}{2}-\frac{1}{2^{n+1}}\right]\\ &= \frac{2}{2}-\frac{2}{2^{n+1}}\\ &= 1-\frac{1}{2^{n+1-1}}\\ &= 1-\frac{1}{2^n}\end{aligned}$$

The total distance, then, is

$$\lim_{n\to\infty}\left[1-\frac{1}{2^n}\right]=1\,\text{mile}$$

And so the total distance is traversed.